"Man in the Maze"

Table of Contents

Table of Contents (continued)

About the Author

This book is dedicated to
Hazel Rivers, a Salt River
Prayer Warrior and my
constant, long-time best friend.

Acknowledgments

The author wishes to extend thanks and appreciation to the following people:

- ➤ Barbara Johnson, Salt River Tribal Linguist who helped me with all the O'odham words and meanings.
- ➤ Phil Smith, who created and produced the original art work and cover design.
- ➤ Rob Peck, who helped me with the first editing process.
- ➤ Paul McNeese, my final editor and the book's interior designer, without whose professional expertise, constant support, and informed guidance this book might never have happened.

Finally, great thanks to all the Native American People who befriended me and whose stories make this book sing its song.

Preface

For more than fifty years, the Indigenous People of America have been a big part of my life.

My long career in Indian education introduced me to Native Americans, and I soon discovered that Indian people live in two different worlds.

Since 1963 the spirituality and humor from both the Indian and non-Indian world has permeated my world, and in this book I have attempted to bring the best of both worlds together to tell my story and share my philosophy of life.

For 23 years, I taught a Native American Personal Development class at Scottsdale Community College. Reuben Norris, an Apache Pima friend of mine, often spoke to my students. In his honor, I'd like to preface this book with the wise words he often shared with them:

> *"If you're here to judge,*
> *there is nothing I can say that's right,*
> *but if you're here to learn,*
> *there is nothing I can say that's wrong."*

Introduction

For a long time, my son encouraged me to write this book.

He'd say, "Dad, you're a very unusual man and you've lived a unique and fascinating life. You need to tell your story."

When I dragged my feet he'd pull out his best incentive. "Dad, come on, if you don't write it, your grandchildren will never really know their grandpa."

That did it. My son knew that, at the deepest level, his father's love for his ten beautiful grandchildren would motivate him to share his adventures and stories. Each time I got tired of writing I thought of these children and how the lessons in these stories will help them better understand, appreciate and cope with life. I wanted them to know what I know. I still do.

So I hope my story will add value to their lives.

But getting there was a bumpy journey with lots of dead ends. Over the past seven years there were lots of starts and stops. As I wrote, I often became tired, even weary. Who knew that writing would be such a hard job? Everything hurt. My hands, wrists, shoulders—even my brain hurt. I just wanted to give up. But in my mind I would see the faces and hear the voices of my grandchildren. To get my courage back I'd repeat their names and I prayed for help. As I pictured them, new energy and enthusiasm would return and I would begin to write again. I'm convinced it was my love for my wonderful grandchildren, and their love for me, that gave me the vision and determination I needed. I devote this work to each of them!

Chapter 1

The Little Yellow Duck

I grew up in Ohio and, for the first four years of my life, my grandmother—who was from Romania—took care of me.

Then, when my mother re-married, she and my step-dad came and got me and introduced me to my new Grandma, my step-dad's mother. She is the one who taught me about Native American people. A wise woman who had a curiosity about life, a twinkle in her eye, and a confident grin, she was a good cook, loved sweets, and had a cluttered, somewhat messy house.

I still remember our very first meeting. I introduced myself by saying, "My name is Stevie Saffron, and I am four years old, and I want a duck."

Before I went home that day she handed me a cardboard box into which she had put a soft, fuzzy, baby yellow duck. She told me, "Stevie, this is for you."

Yes, she won my heart when she gave me that little yellow duck.

What a way for a kid to meet his grandma! We were no longer *strangers*. An instant closeness happened that day and has lasted a lifetime.

My new Grandma's greatest passions in life were animals and children. In her tiny kitchen she had an incubator she used to hatch out all kinds of baby birds. She had a collie dog named Pal that looked exactly like Lassie. And spending time with her and Pal on that hundred-acre farm was the joy of my life.

Grandma always had desserts to share, and she paid attention to me and told me stories. I was her first grandchild, and she loved being my grandma. When I stayed at her house overnight or on a weekend, she would often take me for long walks and teach me the names of various animals by telling me stories about them.

When I was seven years old, she became the first person in my life to hug me and say, *"Stevie, you are very special to me. I love you very much."*

I can still feel her love—and every time I think of her I am blessed.

For instance, I will never forget one special day when we sat and talked on the steps of her back porch. As we looked out over the barnyard, she told me this story:

"You know Stevie, Ohio is an Indian word that means 'beautiful'. Right here, where this farm is, a long time ago, lived a people who are called American Indians." Then she said, "Come into the kitchen with me, I want to show you something." Opening a cabinet, she withdrew a little glass dish in which she had some arrowheads. She explained that her son, my new Uncle Bud, had found these arrowheads in the cornfield. One by one, she put them in my hand and said, "Stevie, this is proof that these people lived here. Indians had bows and arrows, and with these very sharp arrowheads they hunted their food."

She let me hold the arrowheads in my hand as we went back out onto the porch. Grandma had my complete attention. She was a great storyteller, and I was totally focused on what she was saying.

"Stevie," she continued, "most of the hills, mountains and rivers around here have Indian names."

That was my introduction to Native American people. It intrigued me that someone had lived here before us, and this curiosity began a profound involvement and interest that would shape my life as an adult. My grandma is gone now, but I am forever grateful to her because her love and her stories live on in my heart and mind.

As time passed, I discovered over and over again that my grandma had been right about Indian influences in our society. As you travel throughout the United States, you will discover mountains, rivers, states and towns, named after American Indians. Little did I know that when I was 16 years old my parents would decide to leave Ohio and move us out west, to Arizona. It was here that I pursued my career in Indian education and have worked with Native people from then until now.

For over 50 years, I have been 'traveling' back and forth between the Indian and the non-Indian worlds.

One of the first things I learned was how Native Americans view life and death. When someone passes away, the Pima will say: *"He's gone on; I'll catch up."* I have also heard other Native Americans refer to this life and death process as "those who have gone on before us." The Hopi people, who live in northern Arizona, say: *"He's waiting for us."* This perspective is a softer way at looking at life and death, and it gives us hope that we will all meet again.

***

Most of the people I have written about in this book have left us; in other words, they have gone on, passed away. But in this

3

book you will get to know them. I'll introduce you to Analita, Judum and Leander, each of whom contributed a great deal to my life. I miss my friends, but by writing about them I honor them—and they live on. You will also meet many other people who played important roles in my life, including Chief Dan George.

Some of the people I learned from I will mention by name. Out of respect, though, others will remain anonymous. I hope that what I share with you will bless you as much as it has blessed me.

When I was nineteen years old I met my biological father for the first time—in San Pedro, California, south of Los Angeles. For the remaining 20 years of his life, my father lived at the YMCA, which is where he died at age 63.

"He's gone on; I'll catch up." I am glad we met, but I wish I had known him better. I'm sure he also had stories to tell about his life. It would have been nice if he had left me a book. Thankfully, because of this book, my children and grandchildren will get a pretty good idea about their dad's and grandpa's lives and adventures. I'm happy to say, I find peace and great pleasure in this!

***

In the Indian way, I am now one of the Elders. With most Indian people, you are considered an Elder when you reach the age of 55 years. On most reservations—and in most tribes— Elders are looked up to.

I like what psychiatrist Viktor E. Frankl said about aging in his famous book, *Man's Search for Meaning*. He wrote, *"I don't mind getting older as long as I can keep maturing."* At one point, when I was really down, his book lifted me up and helped

4

me start my life over again. As long as I live, I hope to keep maturing.

Chief Dan George, from the Coast Salish tribe up in Vancouver, British Columbia, Canada, visited our college in 1976, when he was 77 years old. He expressed his gratitude by saying, *"My heart soars like the hawk."*

When I asked him what this meant, he replied, "It means that when you are very happy your heart is soaring like a hawk way up in the sky."

That's how I feel when I share these stories with you: like I am way up high, flying in the sky.

Later in this book you will learn more about Chief Dan George, who performed in the *Little Big Man* film with Dustin Hoffman.

Chapter 2

The Indian Way

The Salt River Pima Maricopa Indian Community is a beautiful place, and the people are a very beautiful people.

Long ago, during the heat of the Arizona summer, the women went topless and the men wore G-strings. It just made good sense to wear as little as possible in the blistering heat. When they traveled to the Trading Post in the village of Scottsdale they would stop their horses and wagons at a row of trees that formed the border between the town and the reservation. On the branches of these trees hung many pairs of pants and a variety of shirts. They would put these clothes on, then go into town and do their trading. Afterwards, on their way home, they would hang the clothes back up on the tree, to be used by the next group of people to come along.

***

Here is an interesting and humorous story that an Indian fellow shared with me (there will be lots of humor in this book; it's the Indian way).

"When the white man came here, he was all dressed up and was carrying a Bible, while the Indians were all running around half naked. Now, here we are—500 years later—and the white people are running around naked, while the Indians are all dressed up and carrying Bibles!"

***

In 1963, when I was 20 years old, I had a spiritual experience with a power greater than myself that dramatically changed my life. Feeling God's love I was inspired to seek added purpose and meaning to my life by enrolling at Mesa Community College to prepare myself to do something better with my life.

Almost immediately I met Larry Manuel, a Native American Pima student from the Salt River Indian Community. He needed a ride home after class, and I had to drive right through his reservation to get to my home. Thus, I started regularly driving Larry to and from classes, and we became friends. As a result of our friendship I learned many wonderful things about the Salt River Pima Maricopa Indian Community. Larry eventually introduced me to many of the Elders in the community, notable people like Anna Shaw and Billman Hays, Sr.

In fact, as time passed, many of Larry's friends and relatives became my friends and 'relatives'. They were not my blood relatives, of course, but I soon learned a new way of thinking called *"The Indian Way."* I learned that Indian People from various tribes have their own unique cultural ways of seeing and experiencing the world.

First of all, *from a Native perspective, we are **all** related.* Regardless of our ethnic or religious differences, we are all relatives. This is an Indian value that exists even to this day.

Larry and I soon became good friends. I recall how, on one bright, clear spring day, I pointed out to him how beautiful the mountains looked from his house. After a few seconds of silently gazing at the mountains and thinking about what I said, he replied, "I never noticed them until you came along."

I remember another time—a morning when Larry asked me to loan him five dollars. Here's how he eased me into giving him five bucks: He said: "Money and me are strangers, can I borrow five dollars?"

So, that was Larry Manuel. What an honest man! Right up front. I knew what to expect.

Along the way, I also met his brother Vernon, who was seldom at home because he was a student at an Indian boarding school in Riverside, California. Vernon showed me a bolo tie that he had made in his vocational class. It was decorated with a scorpion encased in clear plastic. I said: "This is so beautiful." Then Vernon handed it to me and said, "Here, I want you to have it." He just gave it to me! I will never forget this offering of friendship.

This happened fifty years ago, yet I remember it as though it happened yesterday. From this, and from many other such gestures displayed by other members of the community, I learned that the practice of sharing and giving is also a deep-rooted Native American value.

For me, there is something very spiritual about sharing and generosity, and these two brothers were my introduction to the Indian world. I will be forever grateful to each of them.

And I still have the bolo tie!

Chapter 3

People Becoming Human Beings

It was the Pima People who helped the white settlers survive the climate and live well in the Phoenix desert.

In the early days, the Pima tribe did not call themselves "Pima". This is the uniquely Indian story of how they got their name.

A few hundred years ago, when the Spanish explorers came through the valley area which is now called Phoenix, they asked the native people this question: "¿Como se llama?"— which, in Spanish, means, "What's your name?"

They answered, "Pimach," which, in their language, means, "We don't know what you're saying."

Somehow, Pimach was shortened to Pima—and that's how they got their name.

Actually, they call themselves O'odham, also spelled Au-Authm, which simply means "The People."

Similarly, the Navajo people don't call themselves Navajo, they call themselves Dine (Dee-*nay*), which in the Navajo language, also means, "The People".

It seems that many Indian tribes describe themselves as "people" wherever they exist. A while ago I went to Venezuela, and on a tour of Angel Falls, the highest waterfall in the world, I asked our Indian guide for the name of his tribe. He told me, and when I asked about the meaning of the word, he replied, "The People". You will find this to be pretty much the case with Native Americans around the country—and perhaps throughout the whole western hemisphere.

It is very interesting to me that many Native Americans have institutionalized this belief and have chosen to have their Tribal name be called: The People. This seems to put the whole human race on a level playing field. When you think of it, aren't we all just people trying to find our way though life?

My Native American friend, Tia Bruised Head, the counselor who replaced me when I retired from teaching at Scottsdale Community College, also helped me to further understand this subject.

She told me, "Yes, we are people, but we are people who are striving to become human beings." Then Tia asked me, *"Do you know what makes us human beings?"* I shook my head, and she explained. *"A human being is a person who feels connected to everything."*

Another way of grasping this concept is the indigenous belief that "All Life is Connected/Give Something Back." We are all related, and we are all connected.

As I said earlier, in The Indian Way we are all 'relatives'; we are related to each other—we are all brothers and sisters.

In fact, I recall Chief Dan George saying, in one of his movies, *"There are many people, but very few human beings."*

Chapter 4

Man in the Maze

The Salt River People have a symbol for 'traveling through life'—it is shaped in the form of a labyrinth known as 'The Man in the Maze.'"

My best friend, Gary "Judum" Frederick, helped me appreciate the meaning of this important symbol. Judum is from the Salt River Indian Community and he knew the culture, language and history of his people.

On my birthday some years ago, he gave me a bolo tie in the shape of The Man in the Maze. We often talked about what the man in the maze symbolized. Over these many years I have talked to many people about how they perceive the Man in the Maze. I have learned that this powerful symbol can be looked at in many different ways. Here is how I see it.

In this Maze I see the Creator and I also see myself. We are on this journey together. As I travel this journey of life I will encounter many twists and turns along the way. The purpose of life is to keep growing and learning until we come full circle. At the center is a place of safety, peace and happiness with our Creator."

The late Elizabeth Kubler Ross, author of many books and essays on death and dying, sheds a little more light on the process: She says: *"Life is a school, and death is the graduation. We are here to learn lessons and when we finish learning we move on."*

For decades now her book, *On Death and Dying,* has been a source of empowerment that helps people cope with the ups and downs of life, as well as with the death of loved ones.

Judum encouraged me to be flexible with the use of The Man in the Maze. He said, "We need to make this symbol work for our day and time. Maybe we can use it to figure out how to find the job that is right for us. We may have to search and change and go through many jobs and learning experiences before we find the career that is best for us. It can even be applied to relationships. The Man in the Maze is a powerful symbol that can be used in a lot of ways."

I personally used it to help me write this book. There were many false starts and unexpected stops. I often tripped, fell down and almost gave up. But the image of the maze gave me hope, kept me going. The maze represented a picture of reality that strengthened my faith. It helped me sense a power greater than myself. I knew if I kept on working at it I would find a way to write and produce this book. The maze also helped me understand that anything worthwhile is not easy; it helped me hang in there and not give up.

***

Recently, I learned something new about the Man in the Maze. I often wondered who designed this symbol. This year, at the end of one of my workshops, a young man from Salt River gave me the answer. He approached me after the presentation and said, "The Creator gave the Man in the Maze to our people."

People everywhere seek to answer basic human questions like 'Who are we?' 'Why are we here?' 'What's this life all about?' It seems to me that most people want to make sense out of life and live forever. The Man in the Maze is powerful because everyone can relate to it. But as far as I know, the O'odham people are the only ones who use this symbol to address these essential questions. People from all over the world have spoken and written many words about life's purposes, but very few have symbols as profound as "The Man in the Maze."

As I was writing this book, I began to think about what this symbol means to me—personally. After much thought, I finally accepted that I am, indeed, just like the man in the maze. I have to decide what I want to do with my life. I have to take responsibility for my journey. I have to negotiate all the twists and turns. I am the sum total of all my choices. And the best news is that I am not alone on this journey.

Judum's explanation of the Man in the Maze put me in the driver's seat and empowered me to live my life, tell my story, and write this book.

* * *

A few years ago, two of my friends from Salt River—Hazel Rivers and Gene Andreas—helped me create a support group that was patterned after the Man in the Maze. Hazel appropriately named our group 'Voices in the Maze.'

The purpose of our gatherings was to share laughter, to deepen our friendships, and also to make new friends. First we would eat together, and then we would share together. Our meetings provided a safe place where we could be ourselves and reach out, with respect and in full consideration of situations and feelings, to help each other. We also welcomed guest speakers and the meetings were open to visitors.

Earl Ray was one of the Elders from Salt River who attended our Voices in the Maze meetings. I used to drive Earl to and from our sessions. One evening, as I was taking him home after our meeting, I asked him two significant questions. What he had to say contributed greatly to my understanding and philosophy of life.

I first asked him, "What is the meaning of the Pima saying, *The Earth is Round*?"

He said it in his Native O'odham language: "Jeved O Sikolk."

Then he explained, "You get out of it what you put into it." In other words, what goes around comes around, and what you send out comes back to you.

My second question for my friend Earl was, "As an Elder from Salt River, what are the three most important things you have learned from your culture?"

What he shared with me is very important.

"First," he said, *"Don't be mean to anyone."*

"Secondly," he continued, *"Look for the good in each other."*

He paused, so I asked, ". . . and what about the third thing?"

He thought for a few seconds and then said: *"If you make a mistake—apologize."*

Ten days later, a car hit Earl as he was walking home. Earl has gone on, but he left me—and now you—with an inspirational expression to live by and three great insights about the purpose and meaning of life.

I was blessed by Earl's wisdom and insight that evening—and thankful that he was so willing to share what he knew about his Native culture. When he left us he took an enormous amount of knowledge and wisdom with him.

I never asked him, but maybe he left a book somewhere. I don't know. Nevertheless, I have been glad ever since that I took the time to give him a lift home and to ask him two simple questions.

In return for the lift, Earl lifted me.

A few days later I was honored and blessed to speak at his wake and funeral.

Chapter 5

Two Worlds Are Better Than One

White People know very little about Indian people, but Indian people know a lot about white people.

This is because Native people have to live in two worlds. Most white people in America only live in one world, which is the white dominant culture.

I, on the other hand, have had the rare good fortune to live in both the Indian and non-Indian world. And for me, two worlds are better than one!

As a teacher and counselor in the Indian world I was able to see my own world more clearly—and I was given the opportunity to embrace the best of both worlds. My spirituality and humor were enriched with Native American spirituality and humor. Eventually, the various aspects of these two worlds became one, just like our two eyes become one in sight. It is like having two windows or two perspectives that help us grasp the meaning of life. Dovetailing the best of both worlds gave me balance, much like standing on two legs instead of one.

Living in two worlds increased my capacity to enjoy life, to give thanks, and to establish and maintain a fresh vision on the pursuit of happiness.

Another key Indian concept best describes what I received: I learned *how to be strong in my power*. The following two learning experiences will help explain what I mean.

***

For twenty-five years, I worked as the Director of Indian Services at Scottsdale Community College. One year we were blessed to have two Native Elders come down from Canada to speak to our Indian students. This is the first thing they taught us: *"It's your turn to live; it's your turn to take the culture apart, and put it back together again."*

What a thought provoking and empowering concept!

In their talks, they gave stirring examples of how American Indian people have had to endure their culture and their way of life being taken apart by the white man. Every tribe has its own story of losses and triumphs. Nonetheless, the ability of the indigenous people of America to adapt and change is a great tribute to the fundamental strength, spirit and beliefs of Native People. The very act of reinventing themselves over time to create a new way of life illustrates their resiliency and resourcefulness.

These two visiting Elders then went on to suggest that the culture should be taken apart once more—but with one significant difference: this time, Native people would need to take the lead . . . to be in charge.

Both Elders, in their radical challenge, confronted all of us with the responsibility to take both our individual and community lives apart and put our cultures back together again.

The second thing these two Elders taught us profoundly influenced my life. They said: *"You have power—and you can be weak in your power, or you can be strong in your power."* You can be weak in your power by failing to do something positive with your life, or you can be strong in your power by reaching out, making a difference, and helping the world be a better place."

I have given both of these concepts a lot of thought. I also factored in what I learned from two other Indian men.

***

A Navajo named Raymond Bradley told me, *"The sun comes up every day so that you can learn something."* You will learn more from him later, when I discuss 9/11—in Chapter 12.

The other Native man was Roy Track, who also enlightened me when he said: *"You are the center of the universe."*

Roy's last name was really 'Track in the Woods'. He hosted the longest running Native TV Show in the country. It was called the 21st Century Native American. In his honor, there is now the Roy Track Memorial Pow Wow, which is held each year in Mesa, Arizona.

***

All these learning experiences made me wonder about my own journey. Here are now some of my conclusions.

As the man in the Maze I am on top of the world and at the center of the universe. I have power, and I can be weak in my power or I can be strong in my power. In order to grow and be happy I need to be open to change. I am here for a reason. The Maze teaches me that life is not easy. This is a learning journey. Each day is a chance to learn something new. I am a person who loves to learn. I need to do what makes me happy.

Slowly, I begin to sense what it means *to be strong in my power.*

***

Over the years, I've met and learned much from various Native American Elders. Billman Hayes, Sr., from the Salt River Pima-Maricopa Indian Community, used to come regularly to speak to my classes. He would talk about his Pima friend, Dr. Roe B. Lewis, and how they would take trips down into Mexico. Both men did research on the O'odham people who lived south of the Arizona border in Mexico. These were the ancestors and relatives of the people in Salt River, Gila River, Ak-Chin and the Papago communities that live in Arizona.

The Papago provide a good example of a people who have taken their culture apart and put it back together again. They gave themselves a proper, more appropriate name. They renamed their tribe, calling it the Tohono O'odham Nation, which means Desert People. No longer are they the Papago.

The Pima in Arizona spoke English, and the Pima in Mexico spoke Spanish. But they were both O'odham and were thus able to communicate in their native language. Dr. Lewis also believed that the Native people who built the famous pyramids near Mexico City were directly related to the Pima, as well. One strong clue revealed by their research was the fact that many of the words in their language were also O'odham words.

Billman Hayes shared something that I will never forget. He said, *"It is up to the young people to come to us to learn their culture and not for us to go to them."* Now that I am older, I know why this is true. Because as one ages, it is often more difficult to get around. Even though the mind may be as sharp as ever, the body finds it hard to get up and go.

More importantly, when people come to you for knowledge and advice, their behavior shows a serious desire to learn and grow. It also shows respect. It indicates that they want to learn. And, on an individual basis, it demonstrates that the seeker is willing to make an effort to become a better person. I have learned a great deal from the Elders who preceded me.

The result of this awareness is that I now 'go to school' with everyone I meet. I have learned so much from so many people. I am here to learn— and then to do something good to help the world be a better place. We are learning creatures, and this is an educational journey!

This open approach to life has revealed a whole new world for me. I encourage you to be open, as well, as you move forward on this adventure called life.

Remember, when you go to the Elders, if you come from a place of respect, you will be blessed many times over.

Chapter 6

Don't Do Anything Crazy

I would now like to tell you about another Elder who took care of me when I was a very little boy.

She was my 'other' grandma, and she was there for me during the first four years of my life. She was from Romania. As it turned out, she lived only five miles from my 'new' grandma, the lady who gifted me with the baby duck I wrote about earlier. My Romanian grandmother knew a lot about the hardships of life.

She and my grandpa had no tractor; they used workhorses on their little farm. There was no running water, just a well. Electricity? None. In the winter they had a dirty old coal furnace that kept us warm. There was no heat upstairs, where I slept with my cousin Wally under a foot-thick, feather-filled comforter. It was very heavy, but it kept us warm in the winter.

I still remember the outside toilet with the Sears & Roebuck catalogue. The farm was at the end of a rutted dirt road that had grass growing in the middle. Everything we ate in the winter came from the gardens, orchards and animals that lived on that farm. On the plus side, as I look back—everything was organic!

When I was a very young child, the outdoors of that old farm became my other hundred-acre playground. In my youth, I got to know every square inch of that place. I knew every hornets nest, fox hole, cherry tree, blue-berry bush, and I knew how a rabbit could jump out and startle you when you walked in the pasture field.

All of God's creation caught my attention and curiosity. The same was true of my other grandmother's hundred-acre farm. As a result, nature became a friend of mine that time could not destroy. Nature had a way of teaching me, stabilizing me. I spent all of my time in the woods, pastures and hay and corn fields. My favorite places to play were the corncrib, the chicken coop—and especially the barn. Oh, how I loved to play in *both* of my grandparents' barns. Plus, I must have climbed every tree on both farms. I knew every fruit tree and especially loved fresh peaches, plums, apples, pears and cherries.

My grandma from Romania learned English through reading the Bible.

She and my grandpa came to Cleveland, Ohio, in 1905. She called Europe "Europa" and referred to Romania as "the old country." She knew a lot about the difficulties of life but nothing about American Indians. She had seven kids, and they all had to speak Romanian. If they did not speak, they got the switch from grandpa.

What a way for a kid to learn a language!

Grandma taught me about God, and how to recite the Lord's Prayer.

(I can still hear my Grandpa crying out to God in Romanian as he said his evening prayers late at night in his bedroom.)

When I was 15 years old, Grandma took me aside and, in her broken English, told me a story that has stayed with me forever.

First, she got my attention and looked me in the eye. Then she said: "Stevie, I want to tell you something. You are young now, but as you grow older and as time goes by, many things will happen to you. *I want you to promise me if you ever get in a jam and don't want to go on, don't do anything crazy.* Remember: *This, too, shall pass."*

As I got older, I realized that what she said was true. I came to see the value and wisdom of her story. There are times when life beats us up, times when we feel betrayed, abandoned, lost, used, and all alone—so alone that we want to give up and say, "Stop the world I want to get off."

There were times in my life when I jumped in the cactus and rolled around. I thought I was so cute; even though it hurt, at the time it seemed to make sense.

I've done many stupid things and I have made many mistakes. Rather than give up, I would always remember my grandma's simple advice: *"Don't do anything crazy; this, too, shall pass."*

The key to life is to be patient and to learn from our mistakes. This is how we change and grow and move on. It's an ongoing, never-ending learning process. This is how this man in the maze gets through his life.

There were times when I hung on for a minute, an hour, or a day. And there were even times I had to wait and be patient and hold on for a year or more before things got better. But I made it through—because I didn't do anything crazy. All these insights about living helped me *be strong in my power.* Every day is an opportunity to learn something new.

Over the years, Indians teased me and in a playful, loving way asked me, "Where is *your* culture?" One Indian student told me: *"The good thing about being an Indian is, you don't have to go across the ocean to find your culture."* So I took the initiative and made a diligent search to find the roots of my people.

Just for the fun of it, I searched my grandfather's name on the Yahoo search engine. His name was Ioan Faloba, and he was from Calvesar, which is a small town in the region of Sibiu,

Romania. Because his name was so unusual, I was able to find my roots in "the old country".

Over the last 15 years, I have visited my relatives in Romania three times. When I visited my grandparents' hometown for the first time, I was simply amazed at their lifestyle; many people still used horses and wagons. However, Romania is no longer dominated by Communism, and most of Romania today is becoming much like the modern western world. Romania is a big and beautiful country. I especially enjoyed seeing the many gypsies who are still part of the Romanian culture.

The Romanian people are wonderfully warm and friendly. My cousin Joey, from Ohio, went with me on that first visit, and our relatives welcomed both of us with open arms. They were amazed that we made this long, seven-thousand-mile journey. We truly felt their love, and they made us feel at home.

And as a result of this first trip I learned a Romanian proverb that I like a lot: *"You never know when the rabbit is going to jump out."* In other words, you never know when you are going to learn something new, or when a great opportunity or gift will present itself.

That gift, that opportunity, was precisely what happened to me with the Native American flute.

Chapter 7

The Native American Flute

The Native American flute became a friend of mine.

The Indian flute is friendly and easy to play if you know how. It is one of the few musical instruments that originated in the western hemisphere.

An Indian named John Rainer made me a flute over 20 years ago. I did not know how to play it, so for years it just sat on my shelf as an ornament, —like a person who barely exists, not knowing how to realize or manifest himself. I have come to realize that our life can be just like that musical instrument— looking good on the outside, maybe, but not happy inside.

One of my favorite sayings is: *"Every thing is possible, if you know how."* Years after I was given the flute, I found a music teacher who taught me how to play the Native American flute. I signed up for his class and learned how to play this amazing instrument. I was very pleased to find that my flute could make music—or, more specifically, that I could actually learn how to make it play music. You never know where your blessings will come from. John Vames was the *stranger* who became my teacher. His book is *The Native American Flute-Understanding the Gift*.

I also have come to believe that we will be the same a few years from now as we are today unless we can bring good people and good books into our lives. Good people and good books can

25

inspire us to *be strong in our power* and help us to make good choices. I am glad John Vames came my way. (You never know when the rabbit is going to jump out.)

A few years ago I spoke at the Native American Indian Education conference in Albuquerque, New Mexico. Afterwards, a Hopi man came up to me and thanked me. Then he shared something that made me feel very happy, "Hey, Steve, because of you I now play the Native American flute." He told me I had introduced him to the flute three years ago when I did a workshop with the Hopi Tribe.

See? John Vames helped me and then I helped this young man. That's how the journey goes. We just keep passing the gift along. God uses people to help people through the amazing 'maze' of life. Remember, *"Everything is possible if you know how."*

By the way, you can also learn to play this beautiful instrument. Just go to Amazon.com and type in *Native American Flute* and you'll find several you can purchase at reasonable prices. Plus, the lesson book for some of them comes with an instructional CD!

An Indian fellow once told me the story of how the flute came into being. He said there was a very high branch on a big, old tree, and each year the woodpecker pecked a hole in it. There were eventually six holes in the branch. Over the years, the branch became old and hollowed-out.

Then, one day, an Indian boy was walking in the woods when he heard music coming from way up—high in the sky. He looked up, listened hard, and was surprised to discover that the music was coming from the top of the tree. As he climbed up and got closer, he was amazed to see a branch with holes, and when the wind blew, the branch made beautiful music.

As the boy carefully brought the branch down he knew in his heart that he had discovered something sacred, something special that moved his spirit. Then the miracle moment came. He put the branch to his mouth and blew his breath into it. As he moved his fingers over the different holes, beautiful sounds started to come out. His heart filled up with joy, and he thanked the Creator (and the woodpecker) for this wonderful gift.

There is something truly special about the Native American flute. Each person makes his or her own music when they blow their breath into it. I don't know anything about musical notes and I have no other musical background, but I must tell you, the flute and I have become best friends. We have become one!

To me, the flute is also a metaphor for life. It represents how we are and how we can be. There is music and beauty in all of us. We just have to figure out how to find it and bring it out. I love learning how to do this in all areas of my life!

When I pass by my flute, it often calls out to me, and I just have to pick it up and play it. It soothes my soul and brings me joy, peace and happiness.

As you can see, I am big on little sayings, and one of my favorite sayings fits here:

"A man without music is like a tree without leaves in the springtime."

Learning how to play the flute has brought harmony into my life. And learning how to live your own life is the key to having harmony. Your story is the greatest gift you have. The "ah-ha moment" comes when you realize that *you have the power* to create—and tell—your own story.

Maybe you have wondered and questioned this thing called life. This is the beginning of spiritual curiosity. What you are sensing is, indeed, a spiritual desire.

Just like there's music in the flute, you don't want to die with the music still in you. So, naturally, you wonder if you can be an instrument in the hands of God. You have been told many times that God uses people to help people. You wonder how; you wonder why.

I must tell you that I have wondered about those things, too. Thankfully, during the course of my life, I have met many wonderful people who have helped me appreciate and understand how to deal with life. Here are three stories of how we can be blessed by *strangers*. Hey—"You never know when the rabbit is going to jump out!"

Chapter 8

The Three Blessings

I once had a devastating experience when I worked as an instructor and counselor at Scottsdale Community College.

For some unexplainable reason, a student who was half Indian and half white disliked me, and he made no bones about it. He was very handsome. He could have passed for Marlon Brando. Unfortunately, he wasn't so beautiful on the inside and started spreading bad rumors and untrue information about me.

To make matters worse, many people believed him. He even got other students to band together against me, and soon thereafter he found ways to question my character and behavior with putting stories in the college newspaper. Pretty soon all these falsehoods threatened to assassinate my character.

My picture, along with these nasty stories, appeared on the front page of the school newspaper every Monday morning, circulating the lie that I was ripping off Indian people and taking money from the Pow Wow. This went on for several weeks, and just when I thought things couldn't get any worse, the Scottsdale City Paper also printed an ugly article about me. I felt as though I had been stabbed so many times that my body was filled with holes! The entire time, no one befriended me or stepped forward to help me deal with these rumors. Even some of my co-workers started looking at me funny, and I began to feel completely betrayed.

One day, totally out of the blue, a *stranger* showed up to help me. A young Pima man from Gila River, around 30 years old, came into my office. I had seen him around, but I really didn't know him. He said, "I see you are going through some hard times and I want to share something with you. I have read the paper, and heard some students talking, and I know the things they are saying about you are not true."

He sure had my attention. At last, someone seemed to care and might sense how I was hurting and feeling. I just looked and listened with much relief and gratitude. I felt a blessing coming!

He continued, *"Steve, this is what I came to tell you. They're going to talk about you before you're born, they're going to talk about you while you're living, and they're going to talk about you after you've gone. The most important thing---is what you say to yourself.*

"You know who you are, and you know you're a good person. You know you have done a lot of good to help students here at the college and that's all that really matters."

Those simple words really touched my heart, comforted my mind, and made a huge difference in my outlook. We shook hands, and I thanked him for stopping in. All these years later, I can't recall his name. I only saw him a couple of times, but I'll be forever thankful for how much he helped me. He was the *stranger* God used that day to provide me with comfort and caring. One more powerful example of the truth behind the saying that "God uses people to help people!"

A few weeks later a formal investigation began, under the direction of the college administration, and I soon was completely exonerated. It was a big relief to be vindicated and innocent of any wrongdoing.

At the same time, I humbly recognized that it was the wisdom and advice from that young Pima student that helped me hang in there and stay positive. Thankfully, this turned into an important learning experience that has helped me throughout my life. The lesson I drew from it is that if you get in a jam and are falsely accused, remember who you really are; and, as my grandma taught me, "Don't do anything crazy!"

What's also interesting is that after I was fully cleared, nothing about me being a good guy was put in the school newspaper. Sensationalism sells.

The second blessing happened on an airplane. About four years ago I sat beside a man on a flight to Idaho. He was ten years older than I and was a college professor. He had written many books. We hit it off and liked each other. As we talked, he said: "Would you like to know my four claims to fame?"

I said, "Yeah . . . sure." I knew he was a smart guy, and I couldn't wait to hear what he had to say.

"My first claim to fame is . . . *I don't know.*

"My second is . . . *I need help.*

"And the third is . . . *I was wrong.*

"And finally, my last claim to fame is . . . *Your idea is better than my idea.*"

Once again, God uses people to help people. This *stranger* was my teacher that day. What he shared deeply resonated with me. It gave me instant perspective and direct insight.

He seemed to know who he was. His words taught me to be humble, because the truth of the matter is this:

I only have a thimble full of knowledge.

As I get older, I oftentimes have more questions and fewer answers. With this attitude and those four 'claims to fame', however, I just may have a chance of learning something.

31

***

My third blessing was *being* the surprise *stranger* at a Navajo sweat lodge up in Kayenta, a small Indian town in the four corners area of Arizona. The leader of the sweat lodge was a man I had met four months earlier at the Navajo College in Tsalie, Arizona. When he recognized me, he welcomed me and instantly befriended me.

At the end of the sweat, he said to me: "Steve, you were a *blessing* to us here tonight. The Elderly say that sometimes a *stranger* will come and sweat with you, and that stranger will bring you a blessing. Tonight was one of those nights."

Then he went on to say, "We sweat every Tuesday evening, and you are always welcome. Now we want to sing you a song."

What I received that evening in the sweat lodge will last as long as I live. Truth be told, it was the men in that sweat lodge who brought me the blessing. Later in this book I will share with you the Navajo prayer song they sang to me in the hope that it will be a blessing for everyone.

***

Will Rogers, a Cherokee Indian from Oklahoma, was a great speaker and humorist. He became quite famous for his expression, "I never met a man I didn't like." I feel this same way, too. I love to meet new people, and I am very thankful for all the positive *strangers* who have come into my life.

As you can see, many of the people who have blessed my life have been strangers. I really do go to school with everyone I meet and I believe "God uses people to help people." Each day is an adventure and a chance to grow and learn something new.

Next, I want to share with you some important lessons I learned from one of the Salt River Elders who started out as a *stranger* and ended up as a really good friend.

Chapter 9

Down by the River

My long time friend Analita Smith, an Elder from the Salt River Indian Community, taught me an important lesson about wellness.

She told me about her nephew, a young man who had a serious drinking problem. She had not seen him for over two years—and then, one day, they both happened to be at the gas station at the same time.

He came running over to her and said: "Hi Auntie, it is good to see you."

She greeted him warmly, then said, "Oh, I wondered where you were;

I thought you just went somewhere to get well."

In a creative, gentle way she let him know that she cared for him and was aware of his problem. In a single sentence, she conveyed how much she wanted him to take care of himself and to go somewhere to get the help that he needed.

I've realized that in one way or another, or at one time or another, every one of us will eventually need a place to go and 'get well'. It might be an alcohol problem, as in Analita's nephew's case, or it could be just a difficult simple situation. A few kind words of understanding and encouragement—just long enough for us to be heard can make such a difference.

And yes, sometimes *you* will be the go-to person whom someone seeks out to get well. Listening to someone is powerful. From time to time we all need some comfort and caring. To me, this is what gives life purpose and meaning. Caring is at the heart of wellness, and love is at the center of the Man in the Maze. A place where we feel the loving presence of something greater than ourselves.

I believe this is how the Creator works. God uses people to help people, and often that help will come from *strangers*. So when you have the desire to help someone, act on it. Good desires come from a spiritual place. It's very interesting to note that the word good and the word God are closely related.

We humans can get out of emotional balance. And without this important inner balance we are no longer happy. More than once in my life I have felt lost and alone and did not think I could go on. I've needed some place to go to get well again. Usually, I've just needed someone to talk to. And it isn't always easy to find such a person or such a place—a place where we can heal and feel loved again, a place to get a grip on life and start over—a space to heal and 'get well'!

***

Analita Smith also shared with me how the Maricopa people acquired their name. Many years ago, the Maricopa people had a conflict with another tribe near Yuma, where they were then living. They left and moved on, and for many years were nomadic, roaming through the desert areas of Arizona and what is now the region called Sonora, in Mexico.

As the story goes, the governor of Sonora asked for the name of their tribe. They replied, "We really don't have a name."

So the governor said, "I would like to give you a name. You are beautiful people. You stay in one place for a while, and then you go on to other places as the seasons guide you. Let us call you 'Mariposa', because you are here and there, just like the beautiful butterfly."

Analita explained "That's how our people got their name. Maricopa came from mariposa, which in Spanish means butter-fly." I have since learned the Maricopa call themselves Piipaash. I would like to know more about their history and culture.

***

I remember asking Analita: "Why do so many people respect you and want you to come over and speak to them. Why do they look up to you as an Elder?"

She gave me a great answer. She said, "I learned how to use one word. *I learned how to say 'no'.*"

She believed it helped her take care of herself and prioritize her life. The proper use of this powerful, one-syllable word—*no*—provided her with the power to do what she needed to do (and not to do what she knew she must not do). It helped her know who she was and to know what she wanted. Analita knew how to say yes, but just as importantly, she knew how to say no.

In this life, you have to learn how to say no. Analita helped me understand that in order to preserve your self-respect you need to have boundaries and practice self-discipline. And often, this means saying "No."

Many people can say "Yes." But, sadly, many people can't say "No," so they risk making unproductive or damaging choices and commitments. As a result, their relationships usually suffer and their lives may get seriously out of balance. By saying yes and seeking approval, they give their power away.

***

I will never forget another thing Analita told me: "Steve, I'm going to take you down by the river, and I am going to tell you all of our ways. But you can't tell anyone, because if you do, something will happen to you." And as you can see, I am still here.

Through the years, Analita taught me many great lessons about life, and I am certainly a better person for having known her. She helped me have the clarity and the confidence to say a brave yes, and a firm no. As you continue reading this book, you will learn a lot more from this *stranger* who became my close friend.

Chapter 10

There's A Good Person In There

I remember a thought provoking story that Howard Rainer told me. Howard is a Native American professional speaker who is one of the best motivators and teachers in the country.

One day, on a speaking trip to South Dakota, a local tribal Elder shared with Howard a problem regarding a young Native man who had recently come to the Elder to confess the alcohol addiction that had messed up his life, reporting that his wife had left him, his children no longer respected him, and no one in his family wanted anything more to do with him. Then the man broke down and cried for a long time in the realization that he'd lost it all, and did not want to live anymore.

The old man listened intently to the young man's story. Then he slowly got up out of his chair, walked over and put his hand on the young man's chest. As he tapped on the young man's chest with his fingers he said these words: *"There's a good person in there, let him come out."* I never forgot that story, or something else that Howard shared with me. He said, "Being Indian is a state of mind."

Howard personally inspired me. He said: "As a professional speaker you need to pace yourself so you don't get burned out.

Always pray and ask for God's inspiration." But the most important thing in life is this: "Don't miss your children. Your family is your number one priority. If you do nothing else...in life....remember to be a good father."

This was hard for me to take in, because I really never had a dad. I had to look to my Higher Power for guidance and direction. I had this thing called Father Hunger, and I didn't want my children to suffer the same thing.

Howard's words of encouragement always stayed with me. He truly helped me to be a better man!

***

Here's a story I heard from a taxi driver in Chicago, a tale that further supports what Howard Rainer taught—that there is a good person in all of us, but sometimes it's hard for that good person to come out (especially when drugs and alcohol get in the way).

I had just arrived at O'Hare airport in Chicago. An African-American taxi driver picked me up, and as I was telling him where to take me I could not help to notice the metal protection screen between the front and the back seat. I said to the driver, "This job must be kind of dangerous."

He nodded and responded by telling me that in the past year a couple of taxi cab drivers had been robbed and killed.

I said, ". . . probably over drugs."

He said, "You're right." Then I heard him say something I will never forget. He said, *"Drugs block the plan."*

I asked him to explain.

"Drugs block the plan, he repeated. "God has a plan for every man, and every woman, and those drugs get in there and block the plan." After a short pause, he continued, "People will say, 'this is my life, leave me alone'. What they don't realize is that drugs hurt the whole family, and drugs bring the whole family down."

On that day, my cab driver was the surprise *stranger* who taught me a lesson about, drugs, alcohol and God.

About six years ago, I, too, realized that I had developed a serious problem with drugs and alcohol—a problem that almost destroyed me. In a later chapter (Chapter 38), you will see how I escaped from this dreadful drinking problem.

Chapter 11

The Power Of Spirit

I remember the speech that Chief Dan George gave when he visited Scottsdale College. He told us that prayer was a big part of the lives of his people. He shared that praying was something his people did every single day. In his tribe, he said, they never let a day go by without taking time to stop and thank the Creator.

Most of the Indian people I know practice some form of Christianity. It's amazing to me how Indians seem to be able to take the good from a lot of different places and bring it all together.

A telling example of this is what happens at wakes. Representatives from all the local churches—and people from all walks of life—come to pay their respects and offer their condolences. Amidst this wide variety there is one strong commonality. Everyone seeks to provide comfort with stories, hymns, poems and songs. And at the end of the ceremony, everybody winds up visiting and eating together.

Over these many years, I have endeavored to make sense out of the role of religion in general—and spirituality and Christianity in particular. Many times (as I learned more about myself and my 'two worlds'), I have changed my views about God.

Recently, I asked my son: "What did you learn from me when you were growing up?" His answer surprised me. He said, "Dad, the most important thing you taught me was that *no one has a corner on God.*"

In other words, God cannot be limited to one narrow box. Here are three things I believe about God and that I would like to share with you.

> *First,* I believe that God loves me. A few years ago I was inspired to put these words on my office wall: *"Thank you God for loving me, and for helping me to love myself, despite my weaknesses."* Every time I read this I remember that no matter how hard life gets, I could still count on God's love.

> *Secondly,* on a personal level, Christ makes a lot of sense to me. Jesus fills up the gaps in my life and brings closure to my circle. In Christ I find the joy to celebrate life and the strength to endure whatever hardships come my way.

The story of Jesus is the best story I know. If you have a better story please share it with me.

For now Christ continues to give me the comfort, hope, and inspiration that I need in life. I've also come to agree with Cecelia Fire Thunder, the Oglala Lakota Sioux leader from Pine Ridge, South Dakota, who once said to me, "I don't care how you worship as long as you worship in a good way."

> The *third thing* I believe about God I learned from a Catholic priest, who said, "You can be religious without being spiritual. You can be spiritual without being religious. *And you can be spiritual and religious at the same time.*" In other words, there's no one 'right' way to communicate with God. The Creator hears and speaks all the languages of the world.

In a most creative way, my Hopi friend, Robert Kaye, enlightened me about Spirit. I once asked him what tribe he was from.

He said, "The Tribe of Christ."

I have a special kinship with Robert and nothing will ever change that!

***

Dorothy Lewis and Leonard Carlos, who were from Salt River, used to come over to the college to speak to the Native students. Mr. Carlos, who was really old then, played the drum, and the two of them would sing songs and tell stories about the Pima and Maricopa culture.

After one of their presentations, I asked Dorothy, "How did your people, your ancestors from long ago, build the pyramids that have been found throughout Central and South America? How did they move those big stones into place? They didn't have bulldozers or cranes. The stones weighed thousands of pounds, and are so tightly placed together, you can hardly get a razor blade in between them. How did they do it?"

Dorothy looked at me and said, *"They moved them with their mind."* Her answer amazed me, and I think she was right.

She also said, "The Pima would get up very early in the morning. They would look to the east, catch the dawn, and wait for the sun to come up over the Superstition Mountains or over the Four Peaks. Then they would stretch out their hands and help the sun slowly come up over the mountain." I thought that was so beautiful because it was a way of connecting and being in tune with the Creator. It's a uniquely affecting way for us human beings to feel connected to the whole universe.

There is a short Sioux prayer expression: "Mitakuye Oyasin." It means, "All My Relatives." It reminds us that we are all connected and related. All of us humans, and even the animals and trees and fish and birds, are related to one another.

Each day it's good to be reminded that we are all brothers and sisters. In the Indian way, it makes no difference whether your skin is black, white, red, yellow or brown. We are all related. In the Indian Way, you are my relative. This provocative Sioux prayer symbolizes this truth.

***

I was in the U.S. Army for a time, and I served in Viet Nam for 15 months. Once, in the middle of the night, a Black soldier we all knew came back to the barracks where we were all sleeping. He had been out drinking and had drunk a little too much that night. He weaved his way to each bunk bed and shook and woke each of us, saying, *"We are all children of the same Lord. We are all children of the same Lord."* Deep in his heart, drunk or sober, he knew that we are all related.

***

The Navajo also have a saying I find very inspiring: *"Walk in Beauty, Walk in Balance."*

To have balance and beauty, we need to pray and ask for help. Indian people taught me that prayer is a big part of each day. Chief Dan George put it this way: "Prayer should begin in the morning when you get up to greet the dawn of a new day. A prayer should also be said to thank the Creator for each meal."

The fact is, this is still practiced today. Almost every Indian gathering I go to includes prayer and thanksgiving. I got a keen reminder of this when I was in the Navajo sweat lodge up in Kayenta, Arizona. The sweat lodge leader said: "Steve, pray every day that you will not miss one of the many blessings that the Creator has for you that day."

I have to be honest. I don't always remember to pray. But I can honestly tell you that when I do, blessings really come my way.

I once heard an old man from Pennsylvania say, *"People are a lot like hogs underneath an acorn tree; they never look up to see where their blessings come from."* I think of that as an important kernel of wisdom. I like the way it makes me think about how easily I can forget to look "up." The words he shared keep me humble and thankful.

***

Two of my most spiritual experiences came as a direct result of the teachings I received from my Apache friends way back in 1972.

The White Mountain Apaches, who live in eastern Arizona on one million, six hundred and sixty six thousand acres of mostly Ponderosa Pine forest, know a lot about hunting and fishing. They taught me how to hunt with an attitude of respect. Here is what they told me.

"Before you go out to hunt the deer, you need to say a prayer; you need to send a message to the deer, and thank the deer for coming and giving his life to you, so that you can live."

I took to heart what they said. A few years ago I went hunting in Ohio with my cousin Joey. Remember, he and I went to Romania together. In my very first hour of deer season, I was blessed with a ten-point, 180-pound White Tail deer. My heart was beating fast when this beautiful animal gave his life up for me. To me it was a sacred moment, but I was also scared. Have you noticed that the words *sacred* and *scared* are closely related?

I recalled what my Apache friends taught me, and I stopped and said a prayer to thank the deer for giving his life to me.

Later, Joey told me that he and his buddies, who had been hunting in the woods and fields of his farm for over 25 years, had never shot a ten-point buck.

I had a similar experience when I went fishing on the Sea of Cortez in El Cabo, Mexico. I sent a prayer out to the fish, and soon a 55-pound Dorado, one of the most beautiful creatures in the sea, came and gave his life to me. Dorado, in Spanish, is translated into English as The Golden One.

No one caught anything that day—except for me.

Believe me, when the fish and the deer gave up their lives to me, I was full of thanksgiving. *My heart truly did soar like the hawk.*

These are two powerful spiritual experiences I will never forget. They are prime examples of the power of prayer. I am grateful to my Apache friends who taught me how to respect and appreciate all living things.

***

Indian people have contributed a great deal to my spiritual development. Throughout the years and as a result of living in these two different worlds, my understanding of spiritual matters has evolved and has changed.

While many white people seem to question the existence of God, most Indian people seem to accept God as a 'given'. In other words, they believe that "God just is!"

Native people refer to God in many ways—as God, or as Jesus, or as the Creator, or as the Great Spirit. But the Indian reference to God that I find most inspiring is, "Grand-Father-

Friend." I like this name because it embraces three key aspects of the Divine and expresses the Great Spirit in human terms. The moment I heard the phrase I realized how wonderfully this man related to God and made the Creator easy for us to approach, understand and respect. He was an Elder from the Ute Tribe in Utah, who referred to God as "Grand-Father-Friend.

It is interesting to note that the name for the state of Utah and the Ute tribe are almost spelled the same. That's how the state got its name.

I have heard other people refer to God as "Higher Power" or "Universe." The name I personally like is "The Most High." This name comes from the Old Testament Bible.

I also recall Bob Dylan, on a TV show, referring to God as "The Great Commander."

I believe that whatever name you call the Creator, if your prayer comes from your heart, it will be heard.

Here's one thing I know for sure: You and I are not alone on life's journey. This is a team effort, and God is the captain of our team. Grand-Father-Friend is always there to help us. The Great Spirit will connect with the human spirit. We are people aspiring to become human beings. But there is also a Supreme Being. *It's this partnership that makes us strong in our power.*

In this partnership, as Martin Luther King, Jr. said in a number of his sermons, "*. . . to expect God to do everything and for us to do nothing is not faith, it's superstition.*"

We have to make the effort to include our Creator as we travel on this journey of life. We have to remember to pray and ask for guidance. I am glad I am alive to do this dance and sing this song.

***

One of the speakers who came to our college was Native American actor Rodney Grant, a member of the Omaha tribe in Nebraska. Rodney is perhaps best known for his role as "Wind-in-his-hair" in the memorable movie, *Dances with Wolves.* I'll never forget one line from his talk that really hit home: *"When the Great Spirit made me, the Great Spirit didn't make no junk."*

Rodney reminded us that we all contain something special, something that is spiritually valuable. But some times junky thoughts do interrupt our life. In fact, when that happens, here is what I say to myself to overcome negative thinking:

➢ Give yourself credit for making the effort to strive to be a good person.

➢ Don't beat yourself up any more. When and if you fall or make a mistake, ask yourself what can I learn from this?

➢ Mistakes are how we grow and become more empathetic.

➢ Empathy is putting your self in the other person's shoes, and seeing and feeling life from their perspective.

➢ All of our pain and suffering and despair is a way for us to connect and relate to the whole human family.

***

To sum it all up, the motto I personally live by is this: *"Be gentle, not judgmental."* We need to get out of the judgment business and into the love business. This is what I strive to do, and I encourage you to do the same thing, too.

***

The 58th chapter of Isaiah describes a "fast" I like a lot. It has nothing to do with not eating. Isaiah encourages us to reach out and love each other. And in so doing, he says: ". . . The Lord will help us *ride the high places* of the earth."

When we pray, the Creator strengthens and guides us successfully through the day.

David says in Psalms 138: "When I cried (prayed) out to God, he answered me, and strengthened me, with strength in my soul." Prayer will help us on our journey. As for me, the Psalms of David are my *secret hiding place* and a big source of my spiritual power. It is through David's honesty with God that I get recharged. David has helped me understand my life, accept my imperfections, and find the courage to change and move on.

Chapter 12

September 11, 2001

On 9/11, the fateful day when those aircraft smashed into the twin towers in New York City, I was in Albuquerque, New Mexico, doing a morning keynote for about 200 people from the Navajo Housing Authority.

I was less than 15 minutes into my keynote speech when, to my surprise, I saw the director of the conference and the leader of the color guard coming down the isle to the platform. As I passed the microphone to the director, he whispered to me: "This is not good news."

Then he announced that there had been a terrorist attack and many hundreds of people had been hurt or killed. His announcement took about 20 seconds, and then he gave me back the microphone.

We all were stunned. I didn't know what I could say. But I knew I'd better come up with something; because I had the group for two more hours! Everyone was silent for about ten seconds, even though it seemed like a lot longer. Finally, I said: "I think we need to pray." Then one Navajo woman in the audience said, *"Let's hold hands and pray."*

I led the group in a short prayer. This centered me, and I was inspired to switch gears and talk about what I learned from Dr. Viktor E. Frankl, the man who wrote the book that had helped me start my life over again—*Man's Search for Meaning*

For over three years Dr. Frankl was in four different Nazi concentration camps. In his book he tells us how despite starvation and all manner of deprivation and disease, he found a way to help fellow prisoners find meaning and maintain a positive attitude. His main message is summed up in the following powerful quote: *"Everything can be taken from a man but one thing: the last of the human freedoms—to choose one's attitude in any given set of circumstances; to choose one's own way."*

In other words, no matter how bleak things look we still have the power to pick a positive path.

The insights and upbeat philosophies of Dr. Frankl helped me so much that I ordered and read every book he ever wrote.

As a result, I was able to share the importance of maintaining a positive attitude. I didn't gloss over pain and suffering. I didn't want to sugar coat the difficulty of having to dig deep to discover the meaning and purpose of life. Here is what I recall saying.

"This life is full of changes and we all have to define and redefine who we are. Our identity is continuously evolving. When tragedy or bad times come, we often get lost and end up in an existential vacuum. In this *empty space* we forget who we are or why we exist. If we are not careful, we can become very angry, and lose our way. When that happens we can easily become addicted to drugs or alcohol—and in this depressed state we can even die way too soon."

Then I told them how Dr. Frankl was able to help people stay positive; not to give up, but rather to find *meaning and purpose* in the midst of deep, dark despair.

I shared with them that I learned from Dr. Frankl that *meaning* involves three distinct actions or attitudes:

First—we need to give something back to the world. We need to make or create something that will help the world be a better

51

place. This will give us something to look forward to and a reason to live.

Second—we need to experience truth, love and beauty. This takes place when we love someone and when we take in the goodness of each day. This is what the Navajo prayer about "walking in beauty and balance" is all about.

Third—when we find ourselves in a difficult situation that we can't change, we need not do anything *crazy*.

When it comes to suffering, we need to be brave and suffer the situation with honor and dignity.

When we choose to face our challenges with courage, our positive attitude brings meaning to suffering and allows us to be lifted, transformed and liberated.

The capacity to bear our burden and rise above suffering is what Dr. Frankl calls "Triumphal Heroism." *The survival of the American Indian is one of the greatest examples of triumphal heroism.*

I still remember one of the Navajo Elders at this conference in Albuquerque saying, "Destruction is nothing new to our people; we have been terrorized for hundreds of years."

The conference continued despite the chaos going on in the world around us, and early the next morning I met a very special Navajo man who taught me something I will always remember.

Here is how it happened. I am an early bird and at 6:00 A.M. I was waiting for the restaurant to open. While waiting I met a *stranger,* a Navajo man named Raymond Bradley. We had breakfast together and he taught me something simple that I never forgot. I mentioned this earlier, but it bears repeating. He said that an old man told him, *"The sun comes up every morning so that you can learn something."*

But Raymond didn't stop there. *"Then, for the rest of the day, you can go into the world and do something good with what you learned, using that knowledge to help someone else."*

Thanks to Raymond's teaching, I've discovered that every time I do this I sleep better that night.

And here's the good part: the next day you get to do it all over again!

Raymond's story re-shaped my attitude and helped me become more aware of the reason and purpose of each day. *The magic light of the morning sun sets the stage for a brand new day.* Raymond helped me answer this question: What are you going to do with today?

A little later in our conversation, Raymond shared some hard truths. I found out that he had his arm severely damaged in an electrical accident. As a result, he chose to wear a prosthetic arm. He said that having to do so sent him into depression, so much so that he started to drink heavily. Fortunately, shortly after this, in a moment of grace, a woman came into his life and loved him. He told me that her love helped him stop drinking and live again.

For my part in the conversation, I told him about an Indian friend of mine who also received a new arm. My Indian friend said he thought about getting a white arm, but he went ahead and got a brown one, anyway! We laughed together and I asked him for *a new, funny Indian story.*

Here's what he told me.

Once there was a Navajo mother who gave birth to a little girl. Oh, how she loved her precious daughter. Every day she dressed her up and took her to school. She encouraged her to study and do well. After school she always helped her with her homework.

When the time came, the mother went to the eighth-grade graduation program. Four years later, she attended her daughter's high school graduation. She was so proud of her daughter that she encouraged her to go off to college and become a teacher. Four more years went by, and the daughter called her mom one day and invited her to come down to the graduation ceremony at the university.

The mother was a traditional Navajo woman. She had her hair up in a bun, and she wore the customary squash-blossom necklace. She also wore a long, beautiful dress that went almost all the way down to the floor—but not quite far enough to cover the old pair of tennis shoes she always wore. Of course, her daughter was embarrassed, and no way, no how, did she want her college friends to see her mother wearing those old tennis shoes. So she told her mom to arrive a day early so they could go shopping for new shoes.

The trip to Phoenix marked the mother's first time in the big city. She was nervous from the moment of her arrival because everything was so different from what she knew back on the reservation. Mother and daughter went to the shoe store together, where a bald-headed salesman waited on them. While he was measuring the mother's foot size, mom wasn't paying attention. She was busy looking all around the store. When she finally looked down and saw his bald head, she was startled. Instantly, she was afraid that the front of her dress had somehow come up and that her knee was showing. In her excitement and embarrassment, she over-reacted and quickly put her dress up over the top of the bald man's head!

My special thanks to Raymond Bradley, who gave me two special gifts that day.

Now, I would like to tell you about one of the greatest gifts I ever received from Native American people.

Chapter 13

The Value of Respect

I have good rapport with most Native people, and we like to poke fun at life—and tease and laugh with each other.

This relationship arises out of mutual respect. Also, I don't try and dress up or look like an Indian. I am happy with who I am. This mutual respect has helped me be my own person.

The value of respect probably started way back there with my second grandmother. Thanks to her, I was taught to respect and appreciate all people, including American Indian people. I thank my grandmother for cultivating the gift of respect in me. To this day, her picture is on my bedroom mirror. Just seeing her picture makes me happy and smile.

Also, I deeply appreciate Desmond Tutu, the great spiritual leader from Africa. In just a few simple words he captured the essence of what I most want to share with you. *"I cannot be me unless you are you."*

I admire how succinctly he sums it up. In one short phrase, he gets right to the heart of why it's so vital to be authentic. I strongly agree and am grateful I've always been able to share this kind of respect with Native American people. It is one of the best feelings in the world.

I have reached a point in life where I feel respect towards all people. However, I mostly learned about the value of respect from Native people. Among the many gifts they've generously shared with me, the principle and the practice of true respect has got to be one of the greatest. Real respect is when you don't look down on someone. We all have our dignity as people, and we all need to honor and respect each other as members of the human family. Everyone is related in some special way!

This is why respect is one of the most important values. It enhances our spirit and increases the quality of our life. With respect, we honor one another. Respect helps us follow Earl Ray's simple advice: "Don't be mean to anybody" and "Look for the good in each other" and "If you make a mistake, apologize."

***

A Native woman who was a student in my class added more wisdom to help me understand true respect. She said, *"Do it with us, not for us."* In other words, don't give us the answers, but rather let us listen to each other and come up with the answers together.

Then another student spoke up and added even more insight. *"If you want other people to respect you, you need to respect yourself."* Once again, my students turned out to be some of my best teachers.

***

Over the years, many white people have created various kinds of programs for Indians and then wondered why the people didn't like it, or why they didn't show up or failed to participate. Perhaps it was because Indian people are often quiet and seem shy. White people often take this shyness as a lack of knowing, and they go ahead and do things without Indian input. They simply do not recognize that silence on the part of Indian people is most often a sign of modesty and respect. I have come to believe, if we want to truly communicate with someone, that the virtue of silence is as important, and oftentimes more powerful than words. Silence, listening and respect all go together.

One of my Pima friends, Ms. Jackie Torres, once said to me, "White people talk too much—and they don't know how to fail." On another occasion, she said to me: "I wish you were an Indian." I trusted she meant it as a great compliment, and that's how I took it.

I'm thankful that Indian people have helped me appreciate and *respect* the value of silence. Some people call it solitude. Being quiet and observing life brings insight, peace and power to our souls.

Because of my deep connections with Indian people, I have become very comfortable with silence. I think being with someone and not having to fill the time up with a lot of chatter reflects a special kind of love. It's only in the silence that we can truly capture the other person's spirit and really know each other.

I've learned that when you find yourself in a conversation doing more than half of the talking, you're talking too much. In Psalm 46, David says: "Be still and know that I am God." This short passage reminds us that we need stillness to connect with the Divine. Proverbs 17 puts it plainly: "Even a fool who keeps his mouth shut is thought to be wise."

Two of the most famous authors of all time, William Shakespeare and Mark Twain, also weigh in. With his customary brevity, Shakespeare advises, "Lend everyone thine ear, but few thy voice." Twain, with his celebrated sense of humor, wisely points out: "We have two ears and one mouth, for a reason. We need to listen twice as much as we speak."

Being quiet and still is a powerful virtue. In the solitude of silence we often find peace *and* hear God's voice. Besides, if we shut up, "Talking God" just might show up! (You will learn more about this later). Silence and listening is all about respect. Great things often happen when not a word is said!

Many years ago, an Indian friend of mine was asked to speak to a tribe up in the Yukon Territory in northern Canada. When he arrived, my friend asked them: "How did you hear about me way up here?" They said: "We have our ways." Unlike most white people, Indians don't like the attention placed on them. They prefer the tribe to receive the attention, or even to have some animal receive the credit and recognition. Sometimes, when there is too much attention—or the wrong kind of attention—Indian people will not say anything . . . but they just won't come around anymore.

***

Once I saw a TV documentary on Native people hunting for seals in Alaska. The hunter stood for hours in the cold, waiting beside the hole in the ice for the seal to come up and catch his breath. Then, finally, the moment came and he pierced the seal with his spear. His friend said "Bull's eye!" But instead of receiving the praise, the hunter told his friend, "I nearly missed." A very typical response—Indian people are quick to give the credit to something other than themselves. As an example, you may recall the story, told earlier, how the woodpecker was given the credit for designing the Native American flute.

***

Another way of knowing and *respecting* someone is a handshake. It is interesting to note the great variety of ways in which people shake hands. Oftentimes, with Native people, the handshake will be affirming, yet gentle. A lot of white people may see it as lame and wimpy. The handshake is often misunderstood. Many white people want a hard gripping handshake, one that oftentimes even hurts your hand!

I learned an interesting aspect about the Native handshake from an Elder from Salt River, Gladys Burke. She attended my Personal Development class at Scottsdale Community College when she was 67 years old. At the beginning of the class I asked each student to share his or her personal goals. Gladys won my heart and got my attention when she shared her goal with this surprising answer: *"My goal is to be a better person."*

Gladys was 30 years older than I—and much wiser. Yet there she was, still expressing the desire to improve her self. Interesting! So I was curious, and I thought she would be the right person to explain the meaning of the handshake from a Native American perspective.

She said, *"We shake hands with respect and with real intent. It is our hope that all the love that is in our heart will be conveyed through our hands and be felt in the other person's heart."* Her answer still deeply touches me!

On another occasion, some years later, I asked a Navajo Elder named Phillip Bluehouse, from Ganado, Arizona, about how the Navajo people greet one another and shake hands. He told me that the Navajo people have their own way of doing it. They shake hands and greet each other by saying, Ya'at'e'e'h," which in Navajo means "hello." But then he shared with me its deeper, spiritual meaning, explaining that the full translation of the expression is: *It is heavenly.*

Various cultures have beautiful ways to greet each other. I am reminded of the way people from India greet each other; they bow slightly and, with hands together in a gesture of prayer, and simply say one word—"Namaste"— which broadly translates into this expression: *May the light that is in me greet the light that is in you.* What a wonderful thing to wish for, to be divinely connected with each other. In Japan, people slightly bow as a gesture of respect when they greet each other. Today, more than ever, an attitude of respect is much needed in this world.

With these thoughts in mind, my goal today is to be more conscious of the importance of meeting each other and to more fully appreciate the spiritual connection that can take place in this greeting process.

***

Analita Smith, the Maricopa Elder from Salt River whom I mentioned earlier, once asked me a surprise question that really made me think. She said: "Steve, Do you only work with Indians?"

"No," I replied, "I work with all kinds of people."

She said, "Good, I would really be worried about you if you could only work with Indian people."

Analita's question, and her response to my answer, made me realize the deep respect that Indians everywhere have for all people. By the way, the Native people have names for white people who want to act and look like them. They call them "Wanna-be's."

Over the years, I have heard various white people say, "I was an Indian in a previous life." But in all these 50 years, I never once heard an Indian say, "I was a white person in a previous life." I'll tell you what. Something about that strikes me as pretty darn funny, but with a very serious undertone. As Shakespeare said, "There is truth in jest."

***

One of the Indian students at the college came up with a great idea. He suggested, "So many white people are curious about us Indians (he was a proud Pima), we ought to have a 'take an Indian to lunch' day." It was a clever idea and it sure made us all laugh.

Chapter 14

Native Sounds

To be strong in our power, and to successfully make it through the Maze of Life, we *need spirit, but* we also definitely need *humor.*

Indian people have contributed greatly to my understanding about laughter, humor and play. Joyful fun is the *super glue* that brings the whole human family together.

Native Americans have *sounds* that have made great contributions to my understanding of laughter, humor and play. Long before the white man came, Native people were lifting the human spirit with *sounds* that brought laughter. Sounds such as "Aye!," "K-Yeah!," "Laa!," "Uss!," and "A-ling!, A-ling!, A-ling!"

Here's how my understanding of American Indian humor began. It all started way back in 1972 when I was a counselor at Alchesay High School in Whiteriver, Arizona. Whiteriver is located in eastern Arizona and is the headquarters for the White Mountain Apache Tribe. It's also where the famous Fort Apache is located. *Alchesay* was the name of one of the last great Apache chiefs, and the high school was named in his honor.

The students had a favorite saying: "All the way with Alchesay." I'll bet they're still using that saying today.

Given my position, I had regular contact with every single one of the school's 386 Apache students. At Alchesay, the Apache students would always be laughing and kidding with each other.

In the hallways between classes, you could hear the *sound* of their voices chiming in and saying "K-Yeah!" That's the phrase they'd use after they said or did something funny. When something struck them as humorous they'd all join in together and—in the highest-pitched voices they could muster—they'd all laugh and say "K-Yeah!" I can still hear them doing it! And it always brings a big smile to my face.

The Apache phrase "K-Yeah!"—and especially the way they say it—magically generates laughter within me. Hearing it jump-starts my spirit and makes me feel better.

The joy of happy laughter is essential for everyone's wellbeing. Humorous sounds like "K-Yeah!" or "Aye" or "A-ling, A-ling, A-ling" send a signal to the funny bone that can cause us to lighten up and laugh.

The sound of these words have power. Our perspective is instantly altered and our spirit is lifted. When we loosen up and laugh, we get a new positive energy that makes us feel better.

Laughter is contagious, and these ethnic expressions and sounds prompt us to lighten up. C'mon, try it, say "K-Yeah!" with me. I promise: if you really say it with feeling, the sound will move you. *"K-Yeah!"*

The exact words and/or sounds are uniquely different with each tribe and ethnic group. But the laughter these sounds produce is equally contagious. Every tribe seems to have always had this gift as part of its culture. This was true for the indigenous people of America long before the white man came along.

Recently, after more than 30 years away from my teaching position in Whiteriver, I made a presentation there at a Housing Conference, where I was further enlightened on "K-Yeah!" Before the conference started, I was very fortunate to have an hour's visit with Mr. Ronnie Lupe, who had been the Tribal Chairman for many years and remains a respected White Mountain Apache leader.

He generously shared two examples with me. First, he explained that "K-Yeah!" actually means, *"You did something fantastic!"* For example, if someone rides the bull for eight seconds, many in the crowd watching, with one voice, will shout out, "K-Yeah!" There's just something about those two words that elicit a feeling of happiness and celebration.

See for yourself. Try it with me. On the count of three shout them out. 1 . . . 2 . . . 3 . . ."K- YEAH!" Don't they give your spirit a lift?

As his other example, Mr. Lupe used a basketball game, explaining to me that when someone makes a great pass or shoots from far out and scores a three-pointer, the people in the bleachers will shout (you guessed it), "K-Yeah!" What a wonderful phrase; it makes us smile (at the very least), and it provides a compliment *and* a cheer—all at the same time.

In the same conversation, Mr. Lupe also gave me yet another valuable insight about taking care of the Earth. In the Apache language, the word Ni' (*nick*) is the word for *mind* and it's also the word for *Earth!*

And what is the significance of that dual usage of a single word? To the Apache people, our thought process and our care of the planet are completely intertwined.

I find that very insightful. It's the idea that has inspired me to be more conscious about the environment. We can learn a lot from the Apache culture's practice of using a single word for mind and earth, especially now, while our planet is being so polluted—*by us.* Each day we need to be reminded to give our Mother Earth special care, attention and protection.

***

Analita Smith, my friend from Salt River, also taught me a *sound* to help us lighten up and release stress: She said: "Steve, sometimes you just have to shout out and say "Eee-Yaaa!"

Come on, try it with me. Give this sound a try. "Eee-Yaaa!"

***

Why are all these expressions so important? Because we often keep too many of our feelings inside, where they can back up on us and cause stress and pain. I'm sure you've seen people who are too up-tight. They seem to be emotionally constipated. Studies show that we can be more susceptible to illness and depression if we hold everything in.

***

Now I want to share more examples of the special words or sounds different tribes use to lighten up and laugh. Remember, the Apache use "K-Yeah". The Pima or O'odham people use "Aye".

Aye!" is a special sound, that many tribes use. It's an expression Native people also use to tease each other. But more importantly, it's a word, sound, and gesture that helps people to lighten up and be playful. It is unique and I love it. "Aye!" is probably one of my favorite ways to bring about laughter.

Every culture has its "smile and laugh" words. Our Mexican brothers and sisters, when they are feeling humorous and want to express something funny, they use a slang expression— "Orale!"—which means "lighten up," just the same as "Aye!"

A few years ago, I learned that it also symbolizes something greater. A wise Mexican migrant Head Start leader in Portland, Oregon, taught me that "Orale!" literally means: "to pray to it." In other words, this playful word and sound started out as a spiritual concept. To me, that makes perfect sense because I've always believed that *Humor* and *Spirit* are closely related.

***

A few summers ago I was invited to speak in Bristol Bay, Alaska. I asked the Native people "How do you do it up here? Do you say "Aye!" or do you say, 'K-Yeah?" Right away their faces lit up with a smile. They knew exactly what I was talking about and said, "Yes, we got something, too. We go: "Ah-Ling, Ah-Ling, Ah-Ling" It's so creative and if you say it three times it has a certain power and ring to it.

See for yourself. Try it with me, on the count of three. 1 . . . 2 . . . 3! "Ah-Ling, Ah-Ling, Ah-Ling!"

I just think this is way cool, and for some reason it works even better if you say it three times.

We need to laugh and scream and shout and let our feelings out. Otherwise, unexpressed feelings can turn into trouble. Plus, when we loosen up, our spirits lighten up, and our outlook brightens up.

Chapter 15

Funny Native Stories

Hilda Manuel was a great Pima basket maker from Salt River. She had a wonderful and playful sense of humor. Once she told me a story that still makes me laugh.

"A long time ago," she began, "Pima families lived in 'sandwich' houses. These were small dwellings with very little furniture and few or no items hanging on the walls. Oftentimes, the men wore only G-strings. One evening, two Pima men got into an argument and wanted to hit one another, but there was nothing around the house or on the walls to use as a weapon. Since they could not find anything, they took off their G-Strings and started to slap each other around."

"Ayeee!" Now, that is one funny visual! Thank you, Hilda Manuel.

***

Now let me introduce you to my friend Melvin Deer, Sr.

Melvin was from Oklahoma, and after a few days in town he came over to the college and we put him to work. In no time at all, this *stranger* and I became fast friends. Melvin knew Indian culture, and he also had a great sense of humor and was openly willing to share his funny stories.

I remember one story he told about a ceremony common to many tribes—a "Give Away." When someone passes on, the family gathers up the belongings of the person and gives their personal items away.

At one "Give Away" there was an old woman sitting in the audience. Among the many things to be given away that day was one item that really caught her eye, a colorful bedspread. She had wrapped a scarf around her head, put her hands around the sides of her face, and appeared to be sad and mourning. Every so often she would risk a peek to make sure the bedspread was still there on the table with the other belongings. Finally, she heard someone call out her name. She was very excited as she went up to receive her gift.

There was the bedspread waiting for her on the table. It so happened that she was wearing one of those long, flowing camp dresses with a skirt that went all the way down to the floor. Unbeknownst to her, as she picked up the bedspread and clasped it tightly, she also picked up the entire front of her camp dress. Whereupon she turned completely around, faced the audience, and made this big announcement: "Look at me, everybody, you will never see me like this again!"

***

Melvin was a fantastic teacher and a great storyteller. He was a master at using humor to make a point. For instance, he told me a funny story to illustrate how Indians are fast thinkers.

He started by saying that in order to survive, Native people had to adapt to the many changes that came along—such as the horse in early times, then the white man, and, more recently, the automobile. And the Indian sense of humor helps Native people to be flexible and cope with change.

Okay, you get the point. Are you ready for a fun story? Great, here's Melvin's story.

"My uncle worked the night shift at Tinker Field, an air force base outside of Oklahoma City, Melvin began. "At about two o'clock each morning he would sit down in the same corner, kick back behind some boxes, and take a little siesta.

One night the supervisor came by, and there was Uncle with his head down, just dropping off to sleep.

The supervisor said: "Hey! What are you doing?"

Melvin's uncle thought fast and said, *"Amen."*

Then the supervisor said: "Oh . . . oh, excuse me."

Talk about coming up with a quick recovery. Now that's thinking fast on your seat. Aye!

Melvin also pointed out to me that men from several different tribes share a common—but rather unusual—characteristic. They point with their lips. He said that when the Kiowa men in Oklahoma pointed with their lips they would also be able to say these words: "Whoo-ah-day" which, in Kiowa, means, "Way over there." He told me (with a big grin) that all the Indian girls from nearby tribes were after those Kiowa guys—because they had those "Whoo-a-day" lips! Aye!

Melvin lived in Los Angeles for a while and was responsible for getting real Indians involved in Hollywood movies. In one of the first movies he helped direct, as the ten Indian braves came up over the hill on their horses, the U.S. Calvary fired one shot. The second they heard the one shot, all ten Indian fell down off their horses. Now, there's a funny visual!

I could always count on Melvin for a good laugh. Sadly, Melvin left us much too soon.

The people I miss the most in my life are the people who I laughed with the most in the years gone by. I only knew my friend Melvin for a few years, but his stories are still with me, and my memories of him will last a lifetime. He was like my brother and I miss him a lot. Some day we will 'catch up' and tell more stories, and share more laughs. In the Indian Way, we will all meet again.

Chapter 16

Laughter is Medicine

I think The Creator gave us a sense of humor for a very good reason.

He knew we were going to have to endure some pain and stress. So to help us get through the hard times, He gave us human beings a special gift—the gift of laughter—and the ability to find the humor in tough situations.

As one African-American educator at Arizona State University told me, "If I didn't laugh, I would explode! You'd be seeing flesh and hair all over these walls."

OK, so maybe that's a slight exaggeration. But our lives would surely be a lot more stressful without a sense of humor. If you take life too seriously, you can end up seriously ill. Thankfully, laughter is truly good medicine!

Laughing turns out to be as good for our bodies and our brains as it is for our moods. Studies prove that laughter boosts endorphins and increases healthy blood flow to the brain.

In addition to the physiological benefits, I believe we laugh and have a sense of humor for reasons that are also spiritual. Good humor is designed to lift our spirits, and, as a result, it increases our creativity. It is a gift from the Creator.

God made us so we can laugh. How about that! Every human being, without exception, is born with this capacity. Best of all, laughter is ageless and universal. Everybody laughs—from tiny infants in diapers and booties to little old ladies in tennis shoes!

***

Charlie Hill, an Oneida-Mohawk, was the Warrior of Indian Comedy. He often came to speak at Scottsdale College. One time he made us all laugh when he modified the old Henny Youngman line, saying, "Take my land . . . please!" The simple trick of replacing Youngman's word "wife" with the broader (but just as funny) term "land" was Charlie's creative way of putting a white man's joke into an Indian context, thus revealing yet another great example of merging the humor of two separate worlds into a single, universally funny joke.

Both of these men have gone on, but you can still Google Charlie and Henny and get some really good laughs. While you're on the Google website, see if you can find another master of Indian comedy, an Apache Hopi Tewa man named Drew Lacapa.

Drew once told me, "If only people knew how hard I work to create good humor!" Drew is a master at his craft. His comedy is creative and original. So do yourself a big favor and Google Drew Lacapa. You will laugh until tears run down your leg. Aye!

Charlie Hill, Drew Lacapa and others have paved the way for a lot of Native people to get up on stage and do comedy. Make sure you go to one of Drew's shows if you can.

Again, laughter is medicine and a guaranteed stress-buster that alters our attitude and makes us feel better.

However, words—and the way they're said—have the power to hurt as well as to bring joy. One of my missions in life is to decrease the hurt and increase the joy. I urge you to make it your purpose, as well!

Next, I want to share some of the other important things I know about laughter and humor, ideas I taught in the Laughter and Humor class I led for ten years at Scottsdale Community College.

Chapter 17

The Liberated Laugher

I've learned that while laughter takes place in the body, humor takes place mostly in the mind.

Gilda Radner said, "Humor is the truth . . . only faster!" And Steve Martin puts it this way: "Humor is a surprise."

Then again, I've also heard it described as 'a train wreck in the mind', something that happens when two ideas crash together and out comes something unexpectedly funny. Maybe that's why legendary comedian Sid Caesar commented, "Humor is the truth with a little curlicue on the end of it."

But of all the clever descriptions and quotations about humor, my favorite came from one of our nation's greatest presidents, Abraham Lincoln, who observed, "Laughter is the joyous, universal, eternal, evergreen of life."

Although she's not as famous as Lincoln, I learned much about laughter from the late Dr. Annette Goodheart of Santa Barbara, California. True to her name, Dr. Goodheart was the leading educator in the country on the healing power of laughter. She was a therapist and a healer, and I studied with her for ten years.

Dr. Annette taught me three truths about laughter:

1. You don't have to have a reason to laugh. She showed us how to be "liberated laughers" (her term).

2. You don't have to be happy to laugh. In fact, she quoted the great psychologist and American philosopher, William James, who wrote, "We don't laugh because we're happy, we are happy because we laugh."

3. Laughter and humor are two very different emotions. "Many people who do humor don't laugh," she would say, "but they make *us* laugh."

Dr. Goodheart taught me how to laugh without needing a joke. Thanks to her I am a 'liberated laugher' and can laugh whenever I want to. She also taught that we need to laugh with people, not at people. Dr. Annette Goodheart has now passed on, but I like to believe that in me—and in my work—she lives on.

My great teacher on humor is Dr. Joel Goodman, the Director of The Humor Project in Saratoga, Springs New York. I studied with Dr. Goodman several years ago. He is actually the *founder* of the Humor Project and helps people from around the world focus on the creative power of humor. While working with him I uncovered my humor profile and learned how to become skillful at using humor to promote creativity and learning. I'll be forever grateful to Joel for all the important things he taught me. I'm happy to tell you that Dr. Goodman has a conference every year on humor. To learn more, please visit the following website: http://www.humorproject.com

Humor can be positive or negative. Positive laughter lifts our spirits. It helps us have a positive outlook on life. Good clean fun is essential for the health and wellness of everyone. On the other hand, put-down humor can make us angry and hurt our self-esteem.

Steve Allen, the late, great comedian and writer, said, *"A lot of the humor of our day is lowering the standards of the culture."*

I think he is right. Mean-spirited humor can diminish the goodness of the human spirit. Ridicule is about playing with someone else's pain without their permission. Both approaches—critical humor or sarcastic humor—are forms of verbal bullying.

The word 'sarcasm' comes from the Greek word, sarkasmos, which literally means "to tear flesh." As anyone who's been on the wrong end of a cruel joke knows, humor can heal, or it can kill (in the sense that it hurts our feelings and makes us feel bad about our selves).

A liberated laugher is someone who can laugh anytime they feel like it. They can laugh even when no one else is laughing. When you learn how to do this, you are 'laughter independent'. It is truly possible to do this if you know how. You are in charge of your laugh life. This is powerful medicine.

Norman Cousins, in his best selling book, *Anatomy Of An Illness*, called laughter "internal jogging." He began writing this inspiring book when he was in the hospital with a serious blood disease that made it really hard for him to sleep. The doctors had tried everything in the medical textbook—to no avail. To help cheer himself up, he rented funny movies that made him laugh. To his amazement, he found out that after only ten minutes of laughter he could get two hours of sleep. From that point on, as Cousins reports in his book, he literally *'laughed himself well.'*.

Practicing these tips and tools can bring more laughter into your life. In all my presentations I always say it, and I will say it here: *"A family that laughs and plays together, stays together."*

Chapter 18

Strengthening The Gift Of Laughter

At the end of a Head Start training session in Atlanta, a participant told me, "You're crazy man, but you're crazy good!"

A week or so after the session, he wrote to me:

> *Thank you for strengthening the gift of laughter in our family. We were way too serious, and so hard on our kids to do well in school, that we forgot to play with them. Now I see the benefits of balancing Laughter, Humor, and Play.*

His words meant a lot to me. They also reinforced the importance of teaching people how to lighten up and laugh because it builds family unity and promotes creativity and learning.

I love the sound of my grandchildren's laughter. I especially love it when we laugh together. Stories are fun, and I love sharing funny stories with them. Just as my grandma told me stories and laughed and played with me, I do the same with my children and grandchildren.

The kids are always ready to play. We have fun, and in the process we bond.

Their attention level is high when we're playing, and I am always able to share interesting and memorable stories and ideas. For example, one time I showed up at the door with the Native American flute. As I played the flute, I told them the story about the woodpecker (*see Chapter Seven*), and oh, how they listened—and learned with great intent and anticipation.

Whether it's with my grandkids or with my workshop participants, when we laugh together, we open up and are more willing to learn new things.

I have a playful special *whistle* that my grandchildren love. When I show up at their door I don't knock, I whistle! The minute they hear Grandpa's whistle, they know what's in store and who's at the door. Inside, I can hear them, all excited, saying, "Grandpa's here! Grandpa's here!"

If you think about it, generally speaking, when we whistle we are happy.

Right now, try the whistle test. Whistle with me for a half a minute or so and see if, when you stop, you have a smile on your face.

Whistle 'til you laugh and laugh 'til you whistle. But watch out! One thing nobody can seem to do is whistle and laugh at the same time. I know, 'cause I just tried it.

Remember when you first learned how to whistle? It was a big deal. Well, it still is a big deal. So I encourage you to show up to life armed with a whistle and an active sense of humor. These two things—one an action, the other an attitude—will put more pep in your step.

Maybe someday you'll hear my whistle and it will make you smile.

I now want to give you some more *guidelines to strengthen the gift of laughter*. A primary guideline, translated into three simple letters, came to me from Dr. Goodman during my time at the Humor Project. He calls it the **AT&T** principle; i.e., all the humor we practice needs to be **A**ppropriate, **T**imely and **T**asteful.

He also taught us about what he called: "Humor in a nut-shell," the ten ways for us to bring more humor and laughter into our world:

> ➢ **One liners**
> ➢ **Posters**
> ➢ **Puns**
> ➢ **Cartoons**
> ➢ **Poems**
> ➢ **Funny photos**
> ➢ **Funny gestures**
> ➢ **Funny stories**
> ➢ **Funny Buttons**
> ➢ **Embarrassing Moments**

Look at that last entry. Some of the funniest things happen when somebody messes up. Try telling a funny embarrassing story about *yourself* (or claim it was your cousin!—"Aye!")

***

The ability to do something well is a skill.

How good are you at obtaining and delivering funny stuff?

Humor is a skill well worth developing. Why? Because humor helps us change our perspective, and laughter fights off gloom and depression.

Here's a fun way to develop your sense of humor. Simply *ask people to share a funny story*. Set up a few rules and guidelines for sharing; like only good, clean stuff. Mutual respect is what's needed here; make sure there are no put-downs, or bad words—and no racial or sexist jokes, either.

Everybody laughs at different things. Each person has a very personal and unique sense of humor.

A great way to help you find your own humorous style is to use the above list and the AT&T principle to be your guides.

Keep a humor notebook. Each day, look for something funny. Jot it down, then share what you found with your friends and family. Even at work, and particularly at home, you can sharpen your sense of humor and create a happier environment by setting up a humor bulletin board.

All these skills strengthen the gift of laughter and multiply the chances for a fun ride on your journey of life.

As the saying goes, "A little levity can defy the gravity." It's a great way for people to be happy and *strong in their power*.

Chapter 19

A Splash of Yellow

Here is another strategy that can help you lighten up and stay strong and balanced; in keeping with my last name, Saffron, I call it:
"Putting yellow on your calendar."

This, too, is a skill; and the more you practice it, the more fun and happiness you can bring into your life and to the lives of others.

Before I walk you through the idea, let me tell you how it came about.

For years I'd used red and green Magic Markers to color-code key dates on my calendar. All the speaking engagements I did around the country were noted in red. All my talks at the ten Maricopa colleges were marked in green.

Then, one day when I was with a friend and referring to all those colored markings on my calendar, this lovely, wise lady said to me: *"Steve, where are YOU on your calendar?"*

I looked—and I wasn't there. So she asked me: "Steve, what's your favorite color?"

I thought for a moment and jokingly replied with a line from a famous song by Donovan: "I'm just mad about Saffron, Saffron's mad about me, they call me mellow yellow."

My friend laughed and said, "That's your answer, Steve. You need to put yellow on your calendar *to set aside time for yourself.*"

So I did, and I've been doing it ever since.

The strategy of putting yellow on your calendar is as easy as 1–2-3. Here's how it works:

First, make a list of fun stuff you like to do.

Second, carve out time for it on your calendar.

Third, highlight it with a yellow magic marker. That's all there is to it.

It is the ultimate 'cool tool' that locks in enjoyment time for us, and helps us to remember to balance the work, and play aspects of our lives.

You can even brainstorm fun stuff with your family and friends. As soon as you or somebody comes up with a self-nurturing idea, follow the three steps outlined above. Trust me, it does the spirit good to see fun activities *highlighted in yellow* and scheduled on your calendar. Carving out time for them—and time for yourself—ensures that every week you'll splash around in yellow.

Splashing is fun! I can see you splashing now!

Next, let's bring in the clowns. The Hopi clowns take humor to a deeper, more meaningful and purposeful level.

I have been up to Hopi land many times to see the Hopi clowns. They use playful, humorous antics and skits to make us laugh. At the same time, they also make a point and bring about change. They are brilliant at using humor to get our attention, and equally brilliant at using humor to teach us something profound. The Hopi word for clown is "Tsuku"—which, when translated into English, means *'a sharp point'*.

Chapter 20

The Hopi Clowns

The Hopi Clowns have added a great deal to my understanding about humor.

I am most fortunate to know Allison Secakquaptewa, who has great love and respect for the clowns.

One time, Allison's brother, Emory, shared these insights with me. "The Hopi believe they are living in the fourth world. After they came up and got situated, they began to treat each other with *indifference*. Then the Hopi clowns came. The purpose for the clowns in the Hopi culture is to break up routine, get people's attention, and then teach them something profound."

"Humorous skits, plots and comic antics are used to amuse people so they will be open to valuable lessons that will bring about change.

"The clown society is one of the most sacred societies in all the Southwest Pueblo tribes. Why? Because the clowns are responsible for showing the people their mistakes and where they need to improve as individuals and as a society.

"Throughout the ceremony the clowns wear black and white stripes to point out that they are neither pure nor evil, but a combination of both. During this two-day ceremony, the Owl, Kachina, mysteriously shows up out of nowhere. The Kachina uses a very distinctive sound symbolizing a warning that something terrible may happen to the people if they don't shape up and change their ways. It is quite an amazing ceremony, and it is truly something special to see and be a part of.

"The sacred job of the Hopi clown is to help people examine themselves, and be inspired to make positive changes. The clowns perform various antics or skits on: *"Life as it should not be."* Hundreds of people come out to watch, to laugh, and to learn.

"The clowns act as if they know everything. They have a way of helping their audiences to recognize where they are lagging behind and where they need to improve as individuals and as members of their 'tribe'.

"The clowns seek to awaken all of us and help us see how we need to change our ways so that we can successfully go on with the journey of life.

"To be a clown is a huge responsibility, since the goal of the clowns in this ceremony is to help the people experience an awakening, and because they know there is *a life plan* for each human being.

"To be truly effective, the clowns may stay up all night before the ceremony and pray. And when they go out to educate and entertain the people with their skit or routine, they say this prayer: *"If it be so, may I at least gain one smile."*

"The clown's greatest purpose is to use humor to help us grow and change, so we can experience a happier and more meaningful life. This is a great strategy because if you confront people head on, they won't listen, and if they're not willing to hear you there's no way that they'll make a change. Instead, they feel either intimidated or defensive. So the clowns use fun to get the job done. That is the genius of the clowns. They use humor to get people's attention—and then they teach them something profound.

"The clowns may spend many weeks or months working on a creative humorous skit that has meaning and purpose. Obviously, they get very serious when it comes to creating meaningfully funny routines that will mirror the onlookers and help them see where they need to change and grow. The Hopi clowns have an awesome and sacred responsibility to wake people up so they can change and successfully go on with their journey."

I acknowledge and appreciate both Allison and her brother Emory for sharing this knowledge with me.

***

Each tribe has its own unique sense of humor and its own stories, songs, and rituals that bring perspective and meaning to life. Large head-dresses and unique costumes are often used to make the learning experience more dramatic, so that people will see it, catch it, and derive something from it.

So, I would like to share a few Hopi jokes with you.

Have you heard about the roly-poly Hopi who fell of the mesa? His name was Humpty Dumptewa.

When I was up in Hopi land a Hopi woman told me a good one. She asked, "Why do white people have real long necks and Hopis have real short necks?"

I said, "I don't know."

She laughed and told me: "All those white tourists from all over the world are coming up to see the Hopi, and they are stretching out their necks, wondering where are those Hopis. But those Hopis are all scrunching down and trying to hide from all those white people. That's why Hopis have short necks and white people have such long necks!"

And one time I did a five-hour workshop with about seventy-five Hopi Elders. One of the ladies told me that the Elders are always trying to get the young people to realize the roles they need to play as men and women in the tribe. Then she said: "Reach down and grab that spare tire around your stomach. That's one of the 'rolls' we need to lose."

And now this story, from a Hopi grandmother. One day, her daughter was at work, and grandma was caring for her grandson. She carefully prepared his breakfast, but he wouldn't take a bite. She tried and tried to get him to eat, but nothing worked. Then she had a brilliant idea. She bent her arm, and made a muscle, and said to her grandson: "Look, you need to eat so you get strong muscles." Her grandson looked at her sagging upper arm and said, "Grandma what happened to you?"

Patty Talahongva, one of my Hopi students, would come by my office, not to talk, just to laugh. She would peek around the door to get my attention. We would both smile, and then we would laugh together for a joyful 10 or 15 seconds, becoming "liberated laughers." We could laugh anytime we wanted to, even when nobody said or did anything funny, and no one else was laughing. Then, when she was satisfied, Patty would say, "See you tomorrow . . . Ngey!" (Another sound to make us laugh in Hopi).

Each tribe has its own special sense of humor for bringing laughter to life. For instance, an anthropologist working on the Navajo reservation had decided to learn some Navajo words. As they were riding in the car a roadrunner scooted across the road and the anthropologist quickly asked his Navajo interpreter, "What do you call that?" Without a moment's hesitation, the Navajo linguist replied, "Beep Beep!"

***

When cultures merge or crash together, out comes something funny. Remember—humor is a train wreck in the mind.

Next, a few more examples and several additional opportunities for you to lighten up, have some fun, and laugh out loud with me.

Chapter 21

More Indian Jokes, Aye!

Question: "Are you full-blooded Indian?" Answer: "No, I'm two pints short."

Or, what does one Pima call the other Pima who is shorter than himself? Answer: "Not Even!" . . . Ayeee!

One spring day several years ago, one of my students, Bill Aster, made me laugh when we were sitting in my faculty office at the college. Bill was reading the newspaper. Suddenly, in a very convincing voice, he said: "Look! This period is moving across the paper." I got up to take a look, but just as I got to where Bill was sitting, he said: "Oh no, no, no . . . wait . . . it's just a little bug crawling across the page." It made me laugh, plus it was so original. Now I would like to share with you some more of my favorite funny stories.

***

Many years ago, when I first started to work in Indian Education I asked new students, "What kind of Indian are you?" Usually they would tell me their tribal affiliation. One day a new student came in to register. Sure enough, I asked him that very question: "What kind of Indian are you?

He said: *"A real good one."*

Just now, I added *K-yeah!* His name was Michael Ketchyan, from San Carlos. Michael and I are still friends today, and his answer still makes me laugh! He also gave me an eagle feather, which I still have, and it means a lot to me.

***

My son's favorite Indian joke goes like this:

One day a white guy came onto the reservation. And like a lot of non-Indians, he didn't know his way around. It's easy to get lost, because the streets and roads are not always marked that well. To make matters worse, the directions he got for finding the friend he wished to visit told him to "go past the water tower, take a turn to the right, and there, beside a yellow house, you'll see an old car with weeds all around it. My house is the blue house right behind that house. I got the paint for free, and that's why the house is blue."

So, when the visiting white guy is completely and totally lost, he finally stops his car at a four-way intersection where there is an Indian standing beside the road. He rolls down his window and yells out, "Hey, Indian, where does this road go?"

The Indian thinks a moment, then says: *"Road stay. You go."*

***

One day my office phone rang and a woman's voice, in a low and mysterious tone, said, "Steve, *This is a voice from your past."* That got my attention, but I had no idea who she was. Oh, my gosh, I wondered, maybe it's one of my old girlfriends. Then she broke into a warm laugh and spilled the beans: "Steve, This is Phyllis Bigpond . . . you know, Director of the Phoenix Indian Center." I'd only met Phyllis a few weeks before, so wasn't that familiar with her voice. Boy did she get me! But I'm sure glad she did, because I have pulled the same joke on many people over the years. Phyllis has gone on. She was a great leader and a great lady, and I will always remember her.

***

My secretary at the college was Brenda Phillips, from Salt River. She was not only my secretary, but my true friend for 15 years. She told me this funny story:

Brenda's neighbors were an older couple. The husband, who could not see very well, often got mad at his wife. One day his wife asked him, "Why are you always yelling and getting after me?" He shot back, "You know why. It's because that man comes by every day! He looks right in our back door and stares at you, and you say nothing. Then he goes away" It took the woman a few days to figure out what he was talking about, but finally the light dawned and she sharply told her husband the truth: *"That's no man staring at me; that's the neighbor's horse!*

***

Here's one where it's the wife who mixes things up.

A man attending one of my workshops at Phoenix Indian Hospital shared this true story. He prepared us by saying that his wife often mixes up words.

"Well," said our storyteller, "shortly after he had joined the gym, he overdid it one day on the treadmill and sprained his leg. It hurt a lot, and he came home limping. His wife saw he was hurting and said: "Oh, honey, what happened?" He told her, and she said: *"Oh Baby, put your leg up here on the couch and let it ovulate."*

***

My long time friend, Gene Andreas, from Salt River, and I were talking and in the course of the conversation I said, "Gene, I guess it's an old Indian trick, isn't it?" and then, without a second's hesitation, Gene said: "*And every old Indian's got one.*"

For some reason, that stuck with me, and made me laugh.

Gene is another of my long-time close friends. I recently saw him at a senior luncheon and we talked and laughed together. I remember Gene once telling me this:

"Everyone has a path, and finding and walking our spiritual path is what life is all about." Since Gene is from Salt River, he knows a lot about the Man in the Maze. One thing for sure and I know Gene would agree we have had a lot of good laughs as we have traveled together on this journey of life.

***

Jaa'ii (I pronounce it jaw-ee) is one of my favorite Navajo words because of its meaning, which is *"Donkey Ears."* When children don't listen or misbehave, Navajo parents will correct the child by saying, "Jaw-ee."

So, when you've got someone who's being stubborn and needs to listen, tell them "Jaw-ee!"

I think the sound of the word is pretty funny, and what it stands for is often so true. Practice saying it with me . . . "Jaw-ee!"

You never know when it might be just the right word to use.

***

I recall a funny story I learned from Bob Charette, who's a long-time Native friend of mine living in Billings, Montana. It seems that some Indian kids at the local pre-school were asked, "What is your Tribe? One kid said he was Sioux, the next kid said Cheyenne, and so on. Then the last kid with a puzzled look on his face said: *"I'm Urban."*

***

Hanson Ashley, a Navajo elder whom I greatly respect, shared this funny story with me. He told me to put my fingers together and hold out my hand with the palm facing away from my face. Now, look at your fingers: *They're uneven!* The Creator has a sense of humor."

***

There is one more story I would like to share. It's from Cecelia Fire Thunder, the Oglala Lakota Sioux leader from Pine Ridge, South Dakota. She said, *"God has to be a woman, because no man would put up with all this stuff."* (Only, she didn't use the word stuff . . . Ayeee!)

Laughter is important. It is easy. But pain is another matter. To be strong in our power and to be happy, we need to know how to deal with our painful emotions. This can be a tall order. No one wants to admit they hurt and need healing. Well, we all need to know about the healing of the soul, and laughter almost always helps. But there is another tool we can use to help us heal, get rid of pain, and feel better.

A Portfolio
of
Photographic Memories

These are my grandparents from Romania They came to Cleveland, Ohio, in 1905. This grandma taught me what to do if I ever got in a jam. They took care of me until I was four years old. *Chapter 1*

My American Grandma. She was part Indian, and she introduced me to the Native American People. She taught me that 'Ohio' is an Indian word that means 'beautiful'. When I was seven years old she said, "Stevie, you are very special to me, and I love you very much." This picture greets me every morning because it is mounted on my bedroom mirror. *Chapter 1*

Chief Dan George. Movie actor, writer and poet. A wise and multi-talented Indian leader and one of the last great Chiefs in North America. We all learned much from him when he spent five days with us here—at Scottsdale Community College—deepening our understanding of his world. *Chapter 29*

◆

Chief Dan George's Poem

Love is something you and I must have.
We must have it because our spirit feeds on it.
We must have it because without it, we become
weak and faint.
Without love our self-esteem weakens.
Without it our courage fails.
Without love we can no longer look out
confidently at the world.
But with love we are creative.
With it we march tirelessly.
With and with it alone, we are able
to sacrifice for others.

◆

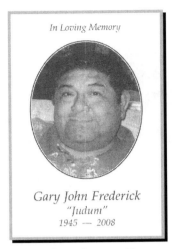

In Loving Memory

Gary John Frederick
"Judum"
1945 — 2008

Judum was my friend and my hero. *Chapter 25* will show you why I feel this way even after he has been gone all this time.

Two of my most valuable possessions are these two bears. Judum wanted me to have his big bear when he passed on. He said, "Steve will know what to do with him." The smaller bear is my Woozhii Bear, and it reminds me of love. *Chapter 25*

In Loving Memory

Earl Phillip Ray
"Lo:dac"
1953 — 2012

Earl Ray knew the Salt River O'odham culture and was a member of *Voices in the Maze*. He taught me three things he learned from his Tribe, as well as the meaning of the expression, "Jeved O Sikolk." *Chapters 4 and 13*

In Loving Memory of
Leander Howard

Born
November 18, 1946
Phoenix, Arizona

Died
January 3, 2008
Scottsdale, Arizona

A Salt River Cosmopolitan man, Leander was one of my best friends. He made me think and look at life from a different perspective. He also told me his explanation of Heaven.
Chapter 32

My ten-point Ohio White Tail Deer. When he gave his life to me, it was truly a spiritual experience. My heart beat fast and I was very grateful. This White Tail Deer reminds me of the power of prayer and how we are all related. *Chapter 11*

I remember the day I said a prayer and went fishing. This fish came home with me and gave his life so I could live my life. Catching the 55-pound Dorado fish on the Sea of Cortez made my heart soar like the hawk. *Chapter 11*

Hazel Rivers is smart and humble. Her every day encouragement kept me going to do this book. This was her master's degree reception. She is the Elder who came up with our study group, *Voices in the Maze.* This book is dedicated to her. *Chapter 4*

Barbara Johnson is the Salt River O'odham linguist. She is a respected Elder and pillar in her community. She knows her culture, History and language. She helped me to find, correctly spell, and understand all the O'odham words. *Acknowledgments*

Back in the day, Brenda was my secretary at Scottsdale Community College—for 15 years! We started out with 27 students and ended up with a staff of five professionals who served over 500 Native American students. *Chapter 21*

Analita Smith and her voice of wisdom is found throughout the pages of this book. The Youth Home in Salt River was her garden. She loved all the children as if they were her very own. She encouraged us to tend the garden after she was gone.
Chapter 40

Allison Secakquaptewa is my dear friend. Here is a picture of her speaking to my Native American Personal Development class at SCC. With passion and profound simplicity she taught us all about the Hopi clowns. *Chapter 20*

Phillip Smith, a Native American born and raised on the Salt River Reservation near Phoenix, contributed mightily to the design of this book. And, in every way, Phil, in training as a graphic artist, demonstrates the main point of my book; that is, **success will happen when you are strong in your power.**

Phil Smith found this design for the "Man in the Maze" symbolism on an old O'odham basket and was inspired to use this version of the Maze on the cover of this book.

Chapter 22

The Healing of the Soul

Life is difficult, and everyone seems to have a fair share of human misery.

Pain can block happiness and cause the music inside us to go silent. Pain is part of life and knowing how to process those emotions is very, very important.

The four painful emotions are:

➢ **Anger**

➢ **Fear**

➢ **Grief**

➢ **Boredom**

If we don't know how to process these four fundamental feelings, they will just keep coming back, causing more pain and trouble.

Most people have experienced some form of abuse, abandonment, neglect, rejection, or betrayal. The term I use for dealing with these painful feelings is called *emotional work*.

From time to time, every person will have to wrestle with one or more of these various painful emotions.

Dr. Frankl, who has greatly influenced my life, points out in his writings an important distinction between the *salvation* of the soul and the *healing* of the soul. The *salvation of the soul*, says Frankl, is a *conversion* experience. You realize the truth of a power greater than yourself. Deep inside, you know and feel that God is real.

I had this experience when I was twenty years old; I chose to accept the realness and truth of Christ, and at that moment I experienced a cleansing and a found a new beginning. However, I also discovered that you don't get it all at the rivers edge, when you are baptized. At least this was not true for me. It was not until some twenty years later that I experienced *the healing of my soul.*

It began in the Navajo sweat lodge which I mentioned briefly in Chapter 8 and will describe in more detail a little later in this book. It was in the sweat lodge that I received a wake up call. I needed an alignment. I needed to go somewhere to get well. I was blessed to find a healer in Santa Barbara, California. The heavy lifting and the big emotional work took place with my healer, Dr. Annette Goodheart, whom you met earlier (in Chapter 16) when we talked about the healing power of laughter. Her therapy helped me face my fears, overcome my anger, and grieve my losses. It was not easy and it took about a year.

I learned that if a lot of emotional and physical damage takes place over many years, especially when you are young, it takes *a while* to process and unfreeze those deep frozen painful emotions. Plus, it takes a skillful healer you can trust. I was very blessed to find a healer to help me heal my mind, body and soul.

Along with Dr. Annette Goodheart, there was another woman who also helped me.

Chapter 23

Changing Woman

As a result of living in two worlds, I was blessed to learn about another source of healing.

The Navajo people introduced me to a legendary woman who also helped me understand and deal effectively with my painful emotions, and to approach the healing of my soul. Her name is *Changing Woman*, and the best way to get to know her is through the many stories she brought to the Navajo people.

For example, there is a practice in the Navajo culture called: *"The baby's first laugh."* Many people still practice this ceremony. Whoever hears the baby laugh for the first time is responsible for bringing it to the family's attention. A big announcement is made, and everyone comes together for a family ceremony and celebration, the central purpose of which is to be reminded of the value and importance of laughter.

***

Life can be difficult, and sometimes we just forget to laugh. I was blessed to meet a teacher named Hanson Ashley who taught at Navajo College in Tsale, Arizona. Having heard that I did workshops on laughter, the first question he asked me when we finally met, was, "Do you know about the baby's first laugh?"

"Yes," I replied, "I've heard about it, but I . . .." I paused, trying to remember.

"Do you know the story behind the baby's first laugh?" he asked.

"No. I didn't even know there was a story."

Hanson told me how the ceremony of the "Baby's First Laugh" began.

"There is always a reason and a purpose for all of our ceremonies.

"Long ago," he explained, "there was a Navajo mother who had a baby, and oh, how she loved her beautiful baby. But her baby was sick. The baby's eyes moved erratically, and the baby was not able to eat or sleep.

"After a couple of weeks of this, the mother was overwhelmed and stressed out with worry. She was at her wits end and totally beside herself, her patience almost gone. Not knowing what to do, she *prayed* and asked for help.

"All of a sudden, she heard the shuffling of feet. Someone was coming. Suddenly, there at her door, was Changing Woman.

"Changing Woman and the baby made eye contact. When this happened the baby started to laugh. And the baby laughed, and laughed, and laughed, until slowly the laughter subsided. Then a strange thing happened. The baby started to cry. The baby cried, and cried, and cried, and finally, when the baby was all cried out, a miracle took place. The baby turned into a beautiful, healthy baby.

Hanson went on to tell me more about Changing Woman.

"Changing Woman brought many wonderful stories to our people. And each story contains valuable lessons to help our people cope with life and be happy and healthy."

***

For me, the *first lesson* from Changing Woman is this: for good health and happiness, we need lots and lots of laughter. Laughter is a great way for us to release our stress and take care of our feelings. The story also teaches us is that prayer and laughter go together! For instance, did you notice how the mother *prayed* and asked for help?

It's interesting to me that there is a Changing Woman, but no Changing Man. Perhaps it's because men typically don't make as much room in their lives for tears or laughter.

Maybe, too, that's the reason most women outlive men. They laugh more, they cry more, they talk more. We men can learn a lot from women about expressing our positive and negative or painful emotions.

And did you also notice the *second important lesson* that Changing Woman brought to the people? First, she showed them how healing it is to laugh. By the same token, she also taught them the value of letting the baby cry and cry, until finally there were no more tears.

Laughter is a coping mechanism for survival and change. It helps us to bend our rigid thinking, to be more flexible—not to be so brittle and to be more open to joy. It enables us not just to survive, but also to thrive. Today, just about everyone has heard and experienced firsthand how laughter is a tool for dealing with stress.

On the other hand, however, *grieving* or *crying* is *a coping mechanism* that we often overlook, which is why it's so significant that Changing Woman shows us that crying is just as important as laughing. She wisely showed us that *both laughing and crying* are essential for our health and well-being. This is a very important lesson and merits our close attention.

Chapter 24

Laughing And Crying Are Cousins

It is important to know that there is more than one way out of sadness, stress and grief.

We have learned about the powerful health benefits of laughter, humor and play. Now it's time to learn about **crying** and **grieving**.

If I gave a talk on crying, nobody would come! So bear with me, because both grieving and crying play a vital role in our health, wellness and happiness. Remember this, if we are to enjoy life and give thanks, we must know how to process even our most painful emotions.

When we're trying to bounce back from a difficult loss, laughter alone is only part of the solution. We have to go deeper to get rid of deep pain. We need to know how to grieve and cry.

Up until now, I have shared with you the important healing benefits of laughter, and now it's important to explain how grieving can help us get rid of stress and pain.

Joy and sorrow have something in common. In many ways, laughing and crying are *the same emotion*. They are cousins! They both provide a healthy *release* that brings *relief*; they are two sides of the same coin.

The chemicals in the tears of crying are different from the chemicals in the tears of laughter. Feelings give off different chemicals. When we hold painful feelings in, these chemicals get backed up. No matter what they stem from, these painful feelings need to come out. Life is about loss, and we need to grieve out these painful feelings. The best cure for grief is grieving. A lot of us simply don't know how to cry. We just cowboy up and act like John Wayne was our Mother. Aye!

A vital part of good self-care is being able to accept the fact that life can be difficult. We may have emotional (and sometimes even physical) aches and pains that we don't understand. We may need a healing ceremony to experience catharsis.

Finding a place to get well is not easy. Healing happens when we get rid of pain and experience an alignment. Catharsis is a cleansing, a purging, and a purification experience. This is what happens in the sweat lodge. It can also happen with a counselor, as well as by sharing openly and deeply with a friend.

If we do this emotional work, the psychological depression and despair, and the physical aches and pains may ease up and be lifted. If we take care of our feelings, over the course of time, the pain will become more manageable, and maybe even go away. However, if it does come back, we will know what it is, and we will have the tools to be able to deal with it. (Plus, we will know that we are not going crazy!)

I like this poem by Ella Wheeler Wilcox:

> *"Laugh and the whole world laughs with you.*
> *Weep and you weep alone.*
> *For the sad old earth must borrow its mirth,*
> *but has trouble enough of its own."*

When we're laughing everyone wants to join us. But when we're filled with sorrow it can often feel like we're on our own. It can be a very lonely place.

When we're feeling down, it is not easy to find someone who will listen and help us grieve out our pain. It takes real courage to admit to someone that we have a problem. I learned firsthand how helpful it can be to have a solid shoulder to cry on.

***

We all need someone with skin on to lean on. I will always remember the Native man who was in one of my workshops. In my session I talked about emotional pain. At the halfway point I made an offer: "If there is anyone here today who is hurting and needs to cry, see me at the break, you can cry with me." Mind you, I had never made this kind of offer before.

Sure enough, an hour later—at the break—a big, tall, barrel-chested Indian man came up to me. In fact, just for the fun of it I said, "Sap Kaic?" which in O'odham means: "How ya doing?" or "What's up?"

He said, *"I am that man."*

I had forgotten all about my offer. But I quickly got serious, and remembered my invitation. I looked at him and sensed his pain. I put my arms around him, and he cried and cried. It was an emotional release for him, and a cathartic healing experience for me, as well.

That was an experience I will never forget—and a lesson well learned.

It's hard to find a space to heal where we can take an emotional risk and let someone know how we feel. This is called being vulnerable. And, if we ask, we may just find someone to hold us, rock us, and soothe away our pain. This kind of love is rare, but oh so important!

Well, now it's time to lighten up and learn a new sound and Native American word that changed my life forever. It's another gift from our Navajo brothers and sisters.

Chapter 25

Woozhii, Woozhii, Woozhii

In addition to Changing Woman, there's another aspect of Navajo culture that has profoundly influenced my life.

It's captured in a single word—**Woozhii**. It's a powerful word, and it's used by both the Navajo and Apache tribes. It means (literally) "tickle."

"Tickle?" Right! Just read on—the 'practical' meaning will come clear in a moment or two.

In fact, I first heard this word in 1977 at the Sunrise Ski Resort in Northern Arizona, which is owned and operated by the White Mountain Apache Tribe. Remember, this is where I started my teaching career at Alchesay High School in 1972.

I had just finished a workshop on college scholarships and we were all standing in line to get a barbecue sandwich. Cynthia Begay and Marie Salt Claw came up to me and said, "Steve, we want to teach you an Indian word that reminds us of you. The word is 'woozhii', and it means *tickle* in our language."

Some Navajo people spell it Wooshie. Either way, the sound of this word resonated with me, and it fits my personality. During the next several years, I took the sound and meaning of the word apart and put it back together again. I transformed the meaning of the word from 'tickle' to something spiritual. To me, *"Our Woozhiiness is our goodness, our playfulness, and our friendliness.*" It represents our spirit of enthusiasm and brings me joy and happiness. To paraphrase the great Negro spiritual: "All God's children got Woozhii!"

Words have power, and the *sound* of woozhii empowered me. Over the years, I continued to add on more meaning, and the more I did, the more it positively influenced the quality of my life.

Woozhii was a gift that kept on giving. It filled a vacuum and rejuvenated my spirit. It truly moves me spiritually! Plus, I have shared it in many of my presentations and it has become a universal sound and concept that seems to make the whole human family happy.

Several years after I learned this word, I found myself up at Navajo College, where a Navajo instructor further enlightened me. I asked him where the word Woozhii came from.

He said, "The coyote brought Woozhii. It seems the coyote was noticing that the spiritual people were getting much too serious and, as a result, they were going to get sick. So coyote introduced them to Woozhii. Coyote knew the power of Woozhii and how it could rejuvenate their spirit in a way that would help them laugh, lighten up, and get rid of stress."

My grandchildren recently attended my Woozhii Workshop at Scottsdale Community College. The Voices in the Maze group sponsored the meeting. It truly was a Woozhii night of fun, laughter and celebration. After I did the workshop, my grandson Andrew—who was eleven years old at the time—said to me, "Grandpa, everything is Woozhii! These are Woozhii lights, and we danced on a Woozhii floor. We are Woozhii people."

My other grandson, Adam, who was seven years old, also came to the workshop to see his grandpa do his thing. Afterwards, I asked him, "What does Woozhii mean to you?" With a big smile, he said to me, "Grandpa, Woozhii is Love!"

Chapter 26

"Judum"—The Bear

Gary "Judum" Frederick got his Indian name later in life.

He knew his culture, language and history, and at his core and in his heart, Judum was really a bear. So, later in life he chose to be called Judum, which is the O'odham word for bear. Not only was he strong—like a bear—but he was also a kind, loving man, and people who knew him thought of him as a great big teddy bear who loved people—and people loved him back.

As you know, Judum was from the Salt River Pima Maricopa Indian Community. He worked at many different jobs through-out the years, and he served on the Salt River Pima Maricopa Tribal Council, as well.

For more than 35 years, Judum and I were best friends. He passed on a few years ago, and I am so glad that we were friends. In an effort to recognize and give thanks for his outstanding influence on my life, I chose to pay special tribute to him by putting a picture of the two of us on the back cover of this book. Plus—in honor of Judum and all of the Native people I have known throughout the years, half of the proceeds from this book will go to Native American students who are pursuing higher education. I talked to Judum's son Isaac, and we both agreed to set up a foundation; it will be called: The Judum Scholarship Fund.

I first met Judum in 1974, when we both worked in the Indian education department at Mesa Public Schools. I still remember when my then-new friend gave me the grand tour of the Salt River Indian Community.

With pride he told me about Chief Azul, who was one of the last great Chiefs of the O'odham People. Antonio Azul was a great warrior who protected his people. The United States cavalry had blue uniforms, and that's how he got his last name. Azul is the Spanish word for blue.

One day, just for the fun of it, I asked Judum a question: "How do you say 'I love you' in Pima?" He answered immediately—"We really don't have a word for I love you, but the closest expression we have is 'I von an sem hohid'."

He translated that phrase as 'I really like you.'

"But," he continued, "if you really, really care for someone, you say, 'Eeeeeee-I von an sem hohid.' And that changes the meaning to 'I *really, really* like you!'

Sometimes, I exaggerate it a little bit and add "I really, really want you baby! Ayeee!

I like that "Eeeeeee!!!" expression because it has to do with intensity of spirit, as well as the measure of energy and passion we must have if we truly care for someone or want to accomplish something great. Over the years, I have taken the liberty to take this word or sound to another level.

The "E-Factor!" helps us grab hold of the real passion and enthusiasm of the human spirit. It's the kind of energy we need to move mountains and accomplish great things. Have you ever engaged in a cause where you had that much passion?

Another way of using this concept is to transfer it to what you are willing to live or die for. No strategy for reaching a great big goal works without energy. Your "E - Factor" symbolizes the energy level needed to mount your willpower, take action, and stay the course. It's a way of measuring and mounting your passion. It embodies the depth of courage that is needed to act in order to bring about change, and it also clarifies what it means to *be strong in your power*. So, on a scale of 1 to 10, we can measure the E – Factor. It takes passion and determination to accomplish something great. To get things done our will power needs to be close to a 10 . This could be used as a simple indicator to expose and express our level of interest and commitment.

Now, I now want to share with you *Judum's favorite funny story*.

"A long time ago there was a young Pima boy who left his village with his bow and arrow and went to the desert to hunt rabbits. He shot a rabbit, picked it up by its ears, and was carrying it back to his village when, all of a sudden, he stopped feeling the weight of the rabbit. He looked down, and to his surprise, the rabbit was walking along with him. He had not killed the rabbit but only knocked it out. When the rabbit came to, the rabbit thought it had made a new friend and was happily walking back to the village with the young Indian boy."

This story was even funnier when Judum acted out the story and told it to me in his Native language. This tale still delights me, and I have honored Judum many times by sharing it with others. Actually, it is an old Pima or O'odham story that has been around for a long, long time.

Judum knew how to live true to his core principles, and he was very good at living and walking in both worlds. Nobody I know could do it better! He took the good from his Native ways and the good from the non-Indian and wrapped it all together like the many strands of a lariat. This is what made him *strong in his power*.

For the last two years of Judum's life, we made a friendship pact to see each other at least once a month. We knew a plan was important because time has a way of slipping away. We had developed a long history, and through the years we helped each other with many different problems as we traveled through the maze of life. We knew we had to keep in touch and meet face to face in order to celebrate life and enjoy our long time friendship. So we would go for lunch and oh, what fun we had as we laughed and ate and told stories.

Now that my friend Judum has gone on, one of the things I miss the most in my everyday life is his laugh. He laughed with his whole body. Every part of him rocked with laughter. It was truly contagious. When Judum laughed, you joined in and were filled with contagious joy right along with him. I thank God for the gift of friendship and laughter we shared together.

I met Judum for lunch about a month before he passed on. By that time in his life he had a prosthetic leg and had gone through triple-by-pass heart surgery, and because of kidney failure he went for dialysis two or three times a week.

I was impressed with Judum's ability to remain joyful and fully alive despite such burdens, and I once asked him, "Judum, how do you do it? How do you manage to stay so positive?"

He smiled and replied, "No one ever asked me that question before." He fell silent for a few moments, thinking, and then, his voice filled with love and respect as he solemnly gave me the answer.

"*I have to thank my parents.* They taught me to appreciate life, to never give up, to have faith, to look for the good in each day, and to give thanks for all my blessings."

Clearly, Judum's parents were the root source of his courage for making it through life's troubles. The love and support he received from his mother and his father helped him *be strong in his power*.

Judum also read my first book, *The First Bird of the Morning*, a 220-page memoir I wrote about ten years ago for my grandchildren to show them who I am and why I believe in God.

Writing has a power of its own. You never know what will appear on the page. That book ended up being a story of my whole life up until that time. Even as I type these pages I can feel that I am in the process of experiencing a new birth. I've got a good sense that this will be one of the best times of my life.

Judum was also the very first person to read the early drafts of this book; he enjoyed both books and was proud of me. He said, "You made me laugh and you made me cry. You made me proud to know you—and proud to be a Native American."

Judum's laugh was contagious, and he was really fun to be around. When we would decide to do something, he would always say, "ALRIGHT," but it was the way he said it—with such passion and energy. He truly was a big teddy bear!

His whole body was full of empathy and passion. He always made me laugh when I called him, because he would tease me and say so convincingly, *"I was just reaching for the phone to call you."* His laugh and his unique expressions always made me smile. I miss that guy! A picture of Judum and me is on my kitchen counter!

Chapter 27

I Have Come Full Circle

In the Indian way, I feel that Judum is in the bleachers of the spirit world, with a lot of my other friends and relatives, wishing me well and cheering me on.

A couple of years before he passed on, Judum gave me a coffee cup with a picture of Indians sitting around a campfire and looking up at the stars. I drink coffee from it every morning. For my birthday, he also gave me a bolo tie with a Man in the Maze design. And there is one other gift that he gave me that really touched my heart. I didn't know about this gift until after he was gone.

The day after his funeral, I went over to his house, and his companion, Sharon, gave me Judum's big old teddy bear. This was *his* bear, the one that he dressed up for special occasions and holidays.

As Sharon gave me this priceless gift she told me that Judum had said, some weeks before his death, that he had come full circle, and if something happened to him she need not to worry because it would just be time for him to go. Judum also instructed her, "If something happens to me, I want Steve to have my Teddy Bear."

Sharon was a little surprised, so she asked Judum: "Are you sure you want Steve to have it?"

Judum answered, "Yes! Steve will know what to do with him."

Judum dressed his bear up for every occasion. When Sharon gave me the bear he was all dressed up in his Halloween costume!

This is truly a special gift, one that I will always treasure. In fact, the Judum Bear now sits on a sofa in my living room. And I am slowly beginning to know what to do with him—I am also sharing him with my grand-children every time they come over to play.

I spoke at Judum's wake, at his funeral, and at his gravesite. I was also honored to grant him one of his final wishes. He very much wanted someone to play the Scottish bagpipes at his funeral. I told Sharon I would take care of it. I searched far and wide and finally found someone.

The distinguished-looking, white-haired Celtic piper, a Mr. Mahony, appeared at the funeral all dressed up in a furry black hat, a decorated black jacket, a flowing blue and green plaid scarf with a matching Highland kilt, knee socks, and—well, he was most definitely the man for the job!

I wanted Judum's funeral to be dramatic, moving, and memorable. I got the idea for how to set it up at a Hopi ceremony, and I outlined my plan to Mr. Mahony in advance.

He was to stay completely out of sight of all the mourners as they arrived. Then, at the beginning of the service, he was to start to play the bagpipes way out in the parking lot. When he began playing, about 150 people inside the Memorial Hall, where the service was being held, began to hear just a hint of the faraway, haunting melody of *Amazing Grace*, certainly wondering where that music was coming from. I, of course, standing at the lectern, was delighted at their wonderment, and I couldn't help but be pleased at the astonishing expressions on so many faces.

Gradually, Mr. Mahony approached the open doors of the Memorial Hall, and the sound grew louder as I stood at the podium, concluding my few remarks.

I knew, of course, what was happening. But I was perhaps the most surprised and emotionally moved of all the people there when the door opened and the Scottish bagpipe player made his grand entry. Just as the Hopi Butterfly suddenly appears at the Tribal ceremonies, it was as if someone from another mysterious, far off world had appeared.

I stood in silence at the podium as Mr. Mahony played, slowly marching across the back of the room and up the side aisle of the Memorial Hall. The eyes of 150 people were fixed on him as I returned to my seat and he made his way forward to stand at the foot of Judum's casket. His timing was perfect. Finishing Amazing Grace just as he arrived at the casket, he allowed only a moment of silence, then played Judum's other favorite song, *How Great Thou Art*.

There was hardly a dry eye in the building. It moves my heart every time I think of it, and when I close my eyes I can still hear the bagpipes playing!

I was so happy to grant Judum his wish. I felt deeply honored that I could arrange the Scottish bagpipes, because I knew it was something he really wanted.

Before he passed on, Judum made plenty of preparations and wanted to be sure that everything, and everyone was taken care of. He even had a special message for his son, Ike, that was left on the young man's computer.

Judum was free-spirited, and he definitely experienced the benefit and enjoyed the fullness of both worlds. He took good from wherever he could find it. He knew how to celebrate life completely.

When the funeral ceremony ended, Judum's casket was loaded onto an old, white pick-up truck and away it went, moving slowly across the reservation, with the pallbearers sitting on both sides of the truck bed. At the gravesite, they lifted the casket out of the truck, and a traditional tribal Elder began singing in his Native language. He sang his songs to the beat of the rattle and the gourd. There were also several other traditional singers present, and they began to sing along with the Elder as they grouped together and followed the casket toward the gravesite. Then, to my surprise, the group stopped, moved to the head of the casket and spread a big blanket out on the ground. The pallbearers gently lowered the casket onto the blanket. There was something woven into—or painted onto—the blanket, but I was far away and could not identify the artwork on it. Then the casket was lifted once again, and the funeral procession repeated this process two or three more times before putting the blanket down in front of the open grave for the last time. Then, having moved closer I could finally see who was on the blanket. It was a big, beautiful, colorful portrait of Elvis Presley!

Judum loved Elvis.

At the end of the burial ceremony, his friends brought Judum's suitcases and some of his favorite personal belongings to the edge of the grave. They put all these things with him so he would have them as he continued his journey.

Judum had an honor guard, as his body lay in state. He was a member of the Tribal Council, and a respected leader in his community. He even worked on the police force. He was also a tribal educator who taught his Native O'odham language classes at the Culture Center, and on his last job he created cultural learning materials.

Gary "Judum" Frederick had truly lived a full life. And, as he said, he had come full circle.

On the way home from his funeral, I could not hold back the tears. When I got home, I fell hard on my bed, and I just didn't cry, I wailed and I wailed, and I cried out to God: "Please, God, help me. I miss my friend Judum. Also, God . . . please bless Judum's family." We all experienced a great loss, and I was profoundly saddened because I had lost my best friend.

Later that evening, I went out to the desert near my house, seeking a place to be alone and to meditate. As I drove across the evening desert I became aware of the faint glow of the full moon coming up over the mountains to the east. In a few minutes it would be coming up over the mountains, known as the Four Peaks.

I remembered how the Pima people used to help the sun up by reaching out with their hands and arms. What they did with the sun, I wanted to do with the moon. So I stopped the car, got out, stood facing the rising moon, and stretched out my arms and with my hands extended, lifting the moon up over the mountains. I thought of Gary 'Judum' Frederick, and I felt connected. My heart filled with thanksgiving for him.

On the way home, a hoot owl with a big wingspan of about four or five feet, swished past my windshield. At first it startled me, but then I took it as a sign that it was time for my friend to leave us and go on. I had never had anything like this happen before.

The best gift Judum gave me was himself and his total, unconditional love and friendship. I can see now how friends are truly gifts to one another. I feel his love and influence just as strongly now as when he was here in person. Judum will never be gone from my life. As a human being, I now realize that we had a rare and wonderful friendship. We knew everything about one other, and we would do anything for each other. I feel that our friendship transcends this world and will last a lifetime, and beyond. I will meet Judum again on some bright, sunny day, and what a joyous meeting that will be.

Meanwhile on a full moon, exactly two months after his death, Judum's companion, Sharon passed on and is now with him on the other side. She was 55 and he was 63 years of age.

Chapter 28

The Kid is Good, Aye!

I hope you have attended one of my trainings, where I always share "The Kid is Good!" routine.

If so, you'll recall that it's about *a very creative way to do positive self-talk.* I use a version of this strategy and a sound to help people lighten up, have fun, and get rid of stress. Because I live in two worlds it's not surprising that "The Kid is Good!" routine has an Indian sound and a 'twist' at the end of it.

This Indian 'twist' ending is almost like a curlicue. It's the part of the expression that serves as both an exclamation mark and a funny sound that makes us laugh. It reminds me of the curlicue on the pig's tail. If you ever need convincing that the Creator has a sense of humor just take a good hard look at the back end of a pig. The way that little tail so cutely curls around it self, now, that's funny!

"The Kid is Good!" routine, coupled with the Indian curlicue, is a great example of why and how I am blessed when two worlds come together. Two cultures are better than one, and double the fun!

If you've never experienced it, here's a way to participate in it. You can try it on for size and see how it fits. It is kind of like the Native American flute—you have to pick it up and play with it. Otherwise, it will stay on the shelf and never make music.

"The Kid is Good!" routine has three parts to it.

First, you need to practice saying, *"The Kid is Good!"* Let's say it together; Here we go, on three: One, Two, Three: "The Kid is Good!" Just for the fun of it, say it three times.

"The Kid is Good!"

Louder with enthusiasm . . .!

"The Kid is Good!"

Great – one more time . . even louder . . .!

"The Kid is Good!"

Wonderful!!

Second, you need to make it more personal and bring it home. To begin, make a fist, put your hand up in the air and point your index finger up—to indicate you are number one. Then at the count of three, point to yourself, and lightly touch your chest. Make sure you really own this next step and make it emphatic by pointing to yourself and saying: "<u>This</u> kid is Good!" All right, here's your chance. Put up your index finger, raise it high (because you're number one). Now point to yourself again, and as you tap your chest, say it *loud* and say it *proud*:

"This kid is good!"

Now comes the *third* part where we put the *positive self-talk formula* all together. This is where we add in the Indian curlicue as a playful exclamation mark.

It's easy. Right after you say "This kid is good!" you playfully add on the sound *"Aye!!"*

So are you ready to put it all together? All right, here are all three parts at once. On three, say it like you really mean it:

One, Two, Three . . .

"This Kid is Good! Aye!"

While saying Aye, and after pointing to yourself, use you hand and make a gesture that extends and swishes across the whole front of your body. It's an act of *celebration* and *confirmation* of your goodness. It's a gift you give yourself!

This is how the Pimas do it. Remember, "Aye" is the sound or expression that the Salt River People use to lighten up, smile, laugh and have fun.

I believe that God works in a mysterious way and the Creator has a special way of blessing us. I believe this because the origin for the "Kid is Good" routine comes from a very unlikely source.

My brother Fritz used to have a drinking problem. Many years ago, he would often call me in the middle of the night. At 2:00 A.M. I would answer the phone half-asleep, and (without even looking at the caller ID panel on my phone) and say, "Hi, Fritz".

He would say, "Steve, I want to tell you something: "The kid is good."

I would say, "I love you man, I know you're a good guy."

And he would say: "No, No, No! You didn't hear me. I want you to know that this kid is good!"

As you may recall, the Romanian people say: "You never know when the rabbit is going to jump out!" And sure enough, you never know when a great idea or opportunity will present itself. Sometimes you see it and grab it right away. Sometimes it takes a few times before you pick up on it. Fortunately, Fritz called more than once with the same message. *Somehow, he knew there was a good person in there.*

Over the years, I have thanked Fritz many times for this gift. He is doing well now and has a wonderfully dry sense of humor. Recently, he told me, "When God made me, He was having an exceptionally good day."

My brother's fun sense of humor made me realize there was more I could add to this routine if I applied some "Yes . . . and" thinking.

If you take The Kid is Good routine and apply some "Yes. . . . and" thinking, you can make it even more playful.

Go ahead. Try a bit of brainstorming with me and see what you come up with.

Do some add-ons.

For example: You can say: "This kid is smart, Aye!" or "This kid is good looking, Aye!" or "This Kid is good at getting along with all the other kids, Aye!"

It is even more enjoyable when you add your own touches and personalize it.

I happily remember the day I did the routine in Minnesota, and my participants added, "This Kid is Good, You *Betcha!*" In Hawaii, they brought their culture into it by saying: "This Kid is Good, *Aloha!*" I got a big laugh one time in Texas, when someone in my workshop came up with: "This Kid is Good, *Yeee-Haaa!*" Then the Hispanic Head Start Migrant workers said, "This Kid is Good, *Orale!*"

Now, how about you, what will you do and say?

I was delighted that various Indian tribes tapped into their different cultures to add their own, unique touch. For example, the Pimas say "This Kid is Good, Aye!" The Apaches say, "This Kid is Good, K-Yeah!" The Zuni version is: "This Kid is Good, Laaa!"

This is what happens when you take from different cultures and add your own touch, as those Native people did in Bristol Bay, Alaska, with: "This Kid is Good, *A-Ling, A-Ling, A-Ling!*"

Chapter 29

Chief Dan George

As the Director of Indian Services, at Scottsdale College I asked the students, "Who is the person you'd most want us to bring to the college to speak with you?"

It was 1976 and the popular film *Little Big Man*, starring Dustin Hoffman, was playing at the local movie theaters. Even though Hoffman was the film's most famous actor and Chief Dan George had a much smaller part, many felt the Chief stole the show.

So not surprisingly, when the votes were tallied, the students had decided that they wanted Chief Dan George to come speak to us. In addition to the student body, two important friends of the college, my pal Royal Arnie Schurz from Salt River, and Gary Judum Frederick, who was the President of the Indian Club, were both strongly in favor of getting Chief Dan George to come to our college for a personal visit. Royal Schurz was the man who was inspired to name the Indian club *The Sun Earth Alliance*.

We had to be resourceful to locate the Chief. But with a little digging, we got his phone number from the Phoenix Indian Center and called him up. Turns out, because of the time zone change, we woke him up at seven o'clock in the morning. Judum just came right out and told him that the Indian students at the college wanted him to come down and spend some time with us in Arizona. He couldn't have been kinder. The first words he said were, "Okay, when do you want me to come?"

Chief Dan George was the Chief of the Tsleil-Waututh Nation, which is a Coast Salish band in North Vancover, British Columbia, Canada. I learned that his full Indian name is Geswanouth Slahoot, which means: "Thunder coming up over the land from the water." But when he was five years old, and first entered the white man's school, that name was too hard to pronounce so they changed it to Dan George. They thought it was important for a young Indian to have a good old, easy to say, American name. That's just the way it was done in those days.

Chief Dan George grabbed our attention the minute he took the microphone. He started his talk by telling us how he got into the movies. He told us that one day, out of the blue, his phone rang. He picked up the receiver and was totally amazed when someone from a Hollywood film company introduced himself and said, "We heard about you, and we want you to play the role of an Indian chief in a movie we are making." The Chief thought for a moment and took a deep breath. Part of him, he said, was excited and wanted to say yes; but another part reminded him that he'd never had any acting experience. So he told the man on the other end of the phone, "Call me back tomorrow at the same time, and I will give you an answer."

As soon as he hung up the phone, the Chief gathered his family together and explained to them that Hollywood called and wanted him to act in a movie. He told his family humbly, and frankly, "I have never been in any movies, and I have no acting experience, What should I do?"

His children gave him this answer: "Daddy, you can do it! Go down there to Hollywood, and show them, that *if an Indian is given a chance, he can do as good as anyone.* Go down to Hollywood and give it a *try.*"

So the next day, at about the same time, the phone rang, and the Chief said just four words to the man from Hollywood: "I'll take the job!"

How Chief Dan George got into the movies is not only a great story, it's a great lesson in wise decision-making. Despite the surprise call and the excitement, the Chief resisted the urge to give a quick answer. Instead, he stayed calm and asked for time to think about it and to talk it over with his family. This process strengthened his confidence to take a risk and helped him choose the right decision.

From start to finish, the story of Chief Dan George's experience in *Little Big Man* shows that when we're brave and take a chance, we never know what amazing things can happen. All we have to do is *try*. But if you don't *try,* you will never know what can happen!

Chief Dan George spent five full days with us at Scottsdale Community College. Every day was another wonderful experience and often included some humor.

One of the funny things that happened was that the Chief had brought clothes for two days, but since it was December—midwinter in British Columbia—and because the weather was so nice and warm here in Arizona, he decided to stay longer. But it got pretty awkward to keep wearing the same clothes. So, I loaned the Chief some of my things. The next thing I knew, the students recognized one of my shirts on the Chief and poked some fun at me: "Steve and the Chief are the same size. Aye!"

At that time, Chief Dan George was 77 years old and had just been nominated for an Academy Award because of his performance in *Little Big Man*. With great leadership, and integrity, The Chief used his popularity and notoriety to promote a better understanding of the First Nations people throughout the United States and Canada. It's amazing how fast word spreads throughout Indian Country. The evening that Chief Dan George came to Scottsdale College, 350 Native people came out to hear him speak.

When the Chief concluded his remarks, there was one man in the audience, and I think it was Byron Sabahe from Salt River, who spoke out in a deep voice. I can still hear him asking in a loud, strong, voice: *"Chief Dan George, must we continue to lose our land?"* When Mr. Sabahe finished his question, the auditorium got so quiet, you could hear a pin drop.

It was clear that Chief Dan George was choosing to carefully think about his answer. After a few seconds of silence, this is what he said: *"From our big land we've been reduced down according to the size of our tribes, and have been given reserves and reservations. Now it's up to us to hold on to the land we now have; it's a reminder that at one time we owned the whole piece."*

It's certainly true that as you travel around America you will find in every state, many places named after various Native Americans. All this is a reminder of a people who lived here long ago—*and who are still here*. This also reminds me what my grandma told me when I was a little boy: "Many of these hills, mountains, rivers and towns have Indian names."

After the Chief gave his powerful answer to Byron Sabahe's question about land ownership, I had a chance to ask what he meant in the movie, when he said, *"It's a good day to die."*

Chief Dan George paused for a minute and then, without any uncertainty, he said in his convincing voice, "It means that as a warrior you are fighting for what is right and good for your people. You are standing up and speaking out for what is just and true. And if you died that day, in the fight for a just cause, it would be a good day to die, because you would be accepted in the eyes of your Creator . . ."

Then the Chief thought for a moment and added: ". . . but maybe, in a couple of weeks, if you were out doing something that was *not* right . . . that would *not* be a good day to die."

The Chief's convincing explanation of this concept presents us with both an inspiring challenge and a firm guideline to live by. It teaches us to treat each day as if it could be our last. And it reminds us that even though we can't control when we'll die, it is fully in our *power* to live each day in a way that honors our best values.

Personally, I would like to live each day of my life doing what I know is right, thus being able to join Chief Dan George in always being able to say, truthfully, *"It's a good day to die!"* I realize this is a lofty thought. But the more fully I live in both worlds, the more fully I find it something to contemplate, aspire to, and live up to.

Later that evening, someone in the audience asked Chief Dan George, "Are you going to write another book?" His answer surprised us and made us smile. He said, "I wrote a book called *Smith* and it was a lot of work. It took me two years to make it up! Then he added with a big smile, "From now on, I think I will just stick with the movies. Movies are a lot less work—and a lot more fun! Plus, a lot of people said I was pretty good in the movies. *And it was up to me to believe them, and I did!"*

Chapter 30

Chief Yellow Lark's Favorite Prayer

Chief Dan George closed his talk to us that night by telling us, "The Native people of this land have always led lives of prayer."

Pausing for emphasis, he then said, "They prayed over everything and they always thanked the Creator.

"Tonight," he said, "I would like to say a prayer for you that is known all over North America. It is called *Chief Yellow Lark's Favorite Prayer*. This is a Sioux prayer, first translated into English in 1887."

"Oh Great Spirit.
Whose Voice I Hear in the Wind,
And Whose Breath Gives Life to All the World.
Hear Me!
I Am a Man Before You.
One of Your Many Children.
I Am Small and Weak,
I Need Your Strength and Wisdom.
Let Me Walk in Beauty,
Make My Eyes Ever Ready To Behold

the Red and Purple Sunset.
Make My Hands Respect the Things You Have Made,
And My Ears Sharp to Hear Your Voice.
Make Me Wise, So That I May Know the Things
You Have Taught My People,
The Lessons You Have Hidden In Every Leaf and Rock.
I Seek Strength, Not That I May Be Superior
to My Brothers and Sisters,
But that I Might Fight My Greatest Enemy-Myself.
Make Me Ever Ready to Come To You with Clean
Hands,
And Straight Eyes,
So That When Life Here Fades, As a Fading Sunset,
My Spirit May Come to You without Shame."

I found this prayer very moving, so I committed myself to memorizing it. It took a long time—and no small amount of effort. I was close to getting it, and I remember working on the ending stanzas over and over again in my mind as I made a long drive to California. I finally got it totally into my memory just before I reached my destination.

Please note in the above prayer I took the liberty to add to the line where he mentions "my brothers" the words " ... and sisters."

This prayer has had a strong influence on how I now view the world. It is no exaggeration to say that learning it by heart changed my life. It took about five hours for me to commit it to memory, but as a result, it has become an important part of my life.

I brought it back with me to my Personal Development class for Native Americans, encouraging each student to memorize this prayer. Then I gave them all a chance to recite it in class for extra college credit. For many years now, I've considered Chief Yellow Lark's Favorite Prayer as a spiritual parallel to The Lord's Prayer, the version of which I know best, reads:

"Our Father, which art in heaven,
Hallowed be thy Name.
Thy Kingdom come, Thy will be done
on earth as it is in heaven.
Give us this day our daily bread,
and forgive us our trespasses,
as we forgive those who trespass
against us.
And lead us not into temptation.
But deliver us from evil.
For thine is the kingdom, the power,
and the glory,
for ever and ever.
Amen!

Each prayer in its own way has proved to be life changing. Once more, I've had the good fortune of drawing from the best of both worlds.

Chapter 31

The Navajo Sweat Lodge

As I've said throughout this book, spirituality and the world of laughter, humor and play cannot be separated.

So I'm glad to follow Chief Yellow Lark's prayer with one of my favorite funny stories. It was told to me by a Navajo woman many years ago.

***

It seems that there were two white ladies who took a trip out to the western part of the country. Neither of them had ever been on the other side of the Mississippi River. On the way, they finally got to New Mexico, where there are several Pueblo Tribes. They heard about the bread that the Pueblo people bake in their traditional outside ovens. The white ladies were hungry, and they eagerly bought a big loaf of the warm, fresh, golden-brown bread. As soon as they got their hands on it they began adding butter and jelly. Well, it was just so delicious that before they knew it, they had eaten it all up.

So, as they continued their trip, driving and driving, always looking for new ovens, they finally left Pueblo Country and found themselves in the Navajo Country of Arizona. They kept on looking for ovens, and finally, they thought they found one.

But what they thought was a Pueblo oven was actually a Navajo sweat lodge!

The Navajo lodge looks like a mound and is made out of dirt and wood, and in a way it really did resemble the Pueblo oven. Sure that they had found a new oven at last, the two excited ladies screamed out, "Look! Look! There's one of those ovens!" They quickly pulled over, jumped out of their seats, slammed their doors, and headed as fast as they could straight for the sweat lodge. The Navajo men who were in the sweat lodge heard the car doors slam, peeked through the flap, and saw the two white women charging right at them! The men were completely shook up and started running like crazy. Then one of the white women, seeing the men take off, yelled out, "Look! Look! gingerbread men!"

***

Several years ago I did a speaking engagement for the high school students in Kayenta, Arizona. After my keynote address I learned that there was a sweat that evening for the men.

The sweat lodge is used in the Navajo culture for spiritual cleansing and purification purposes. So I decided to attend. When I arrived at the lodge, the men were already outside, heating up the rocks. As the men looked up to greet me, I immediately recognized Hanson Ashley, the man who ran the sweat lodge; I had met him about three or four months earlier.

Hanson has now passed on, and he was a wonderful man and a great cultural teacher who taught classes at Navajo College in Tsalee, Arizona.

You may remember Hanson as the man who taught me the story about 'The Baby's First Laugh'.

He warmly welcomed me and we talked briefly about our first meeting. I told him I was new to the sweat lodge ceremony and was worried that the temperature inside the lodge would be too hot for me.

He assured me that I would be able to do it, "Just let the heat go through you one way, and let whatever issues you need to work on go out the other way. The goal is to experience a cleansing and a purification of your mind, body and spirit."

Hanson also told me that one of the symbolic purposes of the sweat lodge is for a man to go back into his mother's womb and be given a chance to start over again. It is a way for a purging and a cleansing to take place. "Hopefully," he added, *"An alignment will happen between you and your Creator. The whole purpose is to release what is bothering you, and to cleanse yourself, so that you can go on with your journey."*

I listened to my friend's words carefully, and I took them to heart.

There was one other white man in our circle.

Then came the moment of truth. It was time to crawl into the sweat lodge. We all stripped down and crawled in.

Fortunately we didn't need to be completely naked. Hanson instructed us two men to put something over our private parts to protect ourselves because of the intense heat. It was so pitch black in the sweat lodge, you could not even see your own hand in front of your face!

Once we had all entered, the Navajo men began chanting, praying, and calling on the Spirit. When the chant ended, Hanson welcomed me and all the other men to the sweat. But it wasn't long before it was just the Navajo guys and me. The other man lasted only one round before it was just too hot for him.

I recall that there were three or four rounds, each about 20 minutes long, and I stayed for each one. Between every round we would go outside, drink some water and let our bodies cool off.

I sensed no 'special' emotions during the first round, but after the first break, at the very beginning of the second round, I started praying. Before long I began feeling some strong emotions. Hansen sensed my spirit and noticed me. He then took a sagebrush, dipped it in a bucket of water, and sprinkled me with some water. Then he also sprinkled water on the hot rocks in the middle of the sweat lodge, which made more steam come up, and that, in turn, made more feelings come out as well.

I got rid of a lot of emotional pain in the second and third rounds, and I began to feel really clean and free. By the time the last round started, I felt deeply cleansed and greatly relieved. A whole lot of painful emotions had revealed themselves, especially negative memories that had to do with my parents putting me down, my real dad leaving me, and my stepdad beating on me with his Navy belt.

Just as the last round was about to begin, Hansen spoke to me as we all sat around the circle of hot rocks. "Steve," he said, "you added a lot to our sweat tonight, and we'd like to sing you a song. Before we sing the song in Navajo, we are going to tell you what the words mean. This is a prayer song for you to take with you."

Hanson explained, "All of the roads out there lead somewhere. As you travel them, you need to be watchful and careful. If you're not careful, you can end up in a ditch with lots of trials and tribulations. Steve, you have your own road to travel, and we Navajo people call it your *journey*. We are going to sing and pray and ask for a blessing to go with you tonight as you continue on your journey. Your road is straight and narrow, and sometimes it will be so narrow that you can't even see it. We are going to ask that *'Talking God'* will be there with you. If you listen, you will hear God's voice. God is like a puppy dog that grows up, and becomes your available, faithful, companion. That's how *Talking God* is."

Then Hanson shared something that was in the prayer song that I still practice each day. He said, "Pray every day that you'll not miss one of the many blessings that the Creator has for you that day."

Then they all started to sing the song in Navajo. I call it the *Navajo Blessing Song.*

It was a beautiful, and moving experience. I do practice the principles revealed in this prayer that remind me to talk to God and to listen for God's voice each day.

I felt blessed by Hanson and all the other Navaho men in the lodge.

When the prayer-song was over, we all went outside, dried off, and got dressed.

Just before we parted, Hanson took the time to share one other thing with me. He said, "Tonight, Steve, you brought us a blessing. The Elderly say that sometimes a *stranger* will come and sweat with you, and that stranger will bring you a blessing. Tonight was one of those nights. We sweat every Tuesday evening, and you are always welcome."

The four lessons from the Navajo prayer song are simply these:

> ➢ *First:* We all have a path and a journey.

> ➢ *Second:* Our journey is straight and narrow and sometimes it is so narrow that we can't even see it.

> ➢ *Third: Talking God* will be there. If you listen you will hear God's voice.

➢ *Fourth:* Pray every day, so that you will not miss one of the many blessings that the Creator has for you that day.

***

Now I would like to introduce you to my friend Leander. He was an original, two-world thinker—a one-of-a-kind, Native American, Pima, O'odham man!

Chapter 32

Leander:
The Cosmopolitan Man

I've told you about my friend Judum, who has had such a lasting influence on my life.

I was fortunate to have a second best friend, a man who also made living in two worlds memorable for me. His name is Leander Howard, and just like Judum, Leander and I were friends for a long time.

One of my enduring memories is of seeing him walking into our Men's Group at Scottsdale Community College. We were a tight circle—seven or eight guys, all from different walks of life, who, for almost three years, would meet every Thursday evening. When he entered the room, we would tease him with his unique-sounding name by greeting him with *"Oh, Leander!"*

Leander was a truly cosmopolitan Indian, a deep thinker who offered many unique thoughts and deep insights to our men's group. He knew his language and his culture as well as anyone I have ever met. For many years of his life he lived on a dirt floor in a traditional Pima sandwich house made out of clay, dirt and wood. In his later years, as his health started to go downhill, he moved over to the Salt River Senior Center, a comfortable place that also had a home for the elderly.

One day, just a few weeks before Leander left us, I felt a strong desire to see him. When I reached the Senior Center I was told that he had become so weak that he had to be taken to the hospital in Scottsdale. Shocked and saddened by this news, I didn't waste any time and went straight to the hospital. But Leander wasn't there; he had not been admitted, and I had no information about who had transported him. Now it was certain that I must find him, so I began checking nearby rehabilitation centers. I went to the first one, which was quite close to the hospital. No luck. But I didn't give up; I drove to the second place, a bit farther away—but they didn't have him, either. Sure enough, at the third center, I finally found my dear old friend. We were both so glad to see each other that it was as if the light in the room had brightened up.

From the moment we met, Leander always had a special way of saying my name. He would take each syllable and stretch out my name in a long, fun-filled way, that always amused me. He said, "Steeeee-vennnnn!" I can still hear how he said it!

The minute Leander saw me, even in his weakened state, he greeted me in this special, grateful way and, as always, it made me smile and feel good. I went to see him two more times after that. But sadly, each time he was unconscious, in a coma, and I was not able to talk to him.

During this first and only visit we talked and caught up on things. I was grateful that he still had his strength and clarity of mind. During our hour-long visit I had the chance to ask him two important questions, things we had never really discussed.

The *first question* was about something I had been asked by a Native American woman whom I long ago heard speak in California.

Here is what she asked, and what I asked Leander to tell me about himself: *"If you could sum it all up in one sentence, what would be the most important thing you learned so far in life?"*

He was silent for nearly a minute—obviously, he was thinking deeply about his response. Finally, looking out the window of his room rather than directly at me, he said just three words: *"APPRECIATE EVERY DAY."*

His answer was short, serious, and to the point. That's all there was to it. And his pointed advice has stayed etched in my head and my heart ever since.

The *second question* I asked him was: *"Leander, do you believe in Heaven?"*

His face instantly softened into a smile, and he said, "Steve, I have thought about that question for a long, long time. I have attended many churches, both on and off the reservation. I have often wondered whether there really is a heaven."

He shifted his body and, for a moment, seemed to drift off. But then he looked at me, fully alert, and continued with his story.

"I used to work at the Indian cemetery in Salt River. I helped bury many of my people, and I often wondered where they went. Then, one day when I was thinking about this, the answer came to me. *They've got to be somewhere because they are not here."*

That was my friend Leander's answer to Heaven. And it was good enough for me.

***

Leander was a master at listening. He spoke slowly and hesitated a lot, especially in conversations with white people. In all the years that I knew him, he often did something peculiar that perplexed a lot of people—especially white people who talked too much; that is, halfway through his sentence, he'd stop talking.

Then he would just look at you in silence, as only he could do, with raised eyebrows and a slight grin, just waiting for you to respond.

Some people thought he was slow, but Leander was actually a very wise man. He knew that if he didn't talk, then you *would* talk, and he could listen—and *learn*. Many times he let you finish his sentences. That way he found out a lot more about you—and about what you were thinking. What was most amazing about this technique is that through his skillful use of silence he was able to have you share everything. And he only had to share a few words. Now, that's some kind of power!

***

Leander was a deep thinker, and there were things that bothered him.

He told me once what hurt him the most. "Many people with money brag and talk about all the fun things they are doing. They tell you about all the places they travel to and they show off all the things they own. They don't realize how much it hurts those of us who do not have the money to do all these kinds of things. It makes us feel envious, jealous, and short changed."

After I heard how much that hurt my friend, I made a promise to myself. From then on, I would never brag about my travels or boast about what I had. It took a great deal of self-determination and self-discipline to keep my word; after all, we all have egos. But I learned from my friend, and I'm proud to say I still practice this wise insight even unto this very day.

Thanks to Leander I learned that it is better to leave some things unsaid. Besides, there are many more important things to talk about than to brag about material possessions or personal accomplishments.

***

I always found Leander to be interesting. He had a way of pointing out to me things that most people don't consider. For instance, he once told me: "Steve, the Europeans did not tell us the whole truth."

I was curious and asked him why.

He told me, ". . . because they ended their fairy tales in a way that we both know isn't true, *"And they all lived happily ever after."* Life has a lot of twist and turns, and as you solve one problem, another one pops up."

***

Leander's life is a good example of a human being living in two worlds. He knew the in and outs of both cultures. Several churches tried to win him over, but none ever did. Leander was a free thinker, who was able to take the good from all sides and remain content within.

When Leander passed on, I had the honor of speaking at his wake. I was also asked to speak at his funeral. After I did, the minister said, "you seem to know him so well, it's okay by me if you also speak on his behalf at the gravesite."

I felt blessed. I knew Leander pretty well, and I think he would have been pleased by the words I spoke and the stories I shared.

After leaving the cemetery, on my way home, I had a spiritual experience of my own. I knew that father time's clock was ticking on my life, too, and Leander's burial brought the truth of death up very close to my door.

As I drove home I prayed. I asked God to help me make the most of the remaining days and years of my life. I asked him to show me the way. I wondered what He wanted me to do with the rest of my time. While praying I immediately became aware of a strong impression that 'Talking God' was speaking to me and saying, *"You be me! You be my hands and feet. You be my voice in the world. Let me love others through you."*

That moment provided a powerful connection that has never left me.

Here's another experience I've had with 'Talking God'. It, too, occurred when I was driving in the car, praying and talking to God, as I often do. I was wishing (praying), "I wish I could be African-American, or perhaps from some kind of an Indian tribe. Or, I wish I knew my own Romanian roots, so that I could be more centered on my native language and in my ethnic identity." Then, it was as if 'Talking God' spoke to my mind in a small, still voice: *"Just be you. I made you so that you can enjoy and appreciate all the cultures of the world."*

Leander reminded me to *appreciate every day.* And what about heaven? For all those people who have gone on, *they got to be somewhere, because they are not here.*

Chapter 33

The Eastern Band

I now want to share three things I learned from the Cherokee people.

In the summer of 2005, I was invited to present a series of topics on Laughter, Friendship and Wellness to the Eastern Band of the Cherokee Indians, in North Carolina. I had always wanted to go there to see the community and to learn more about Cherokee history and culture. The Cherokee people who live in that part of the country, live in the beautiful Smoky Mountains, at a place where two rivers come together.

During the summer months, in a huge stadium that holds a thousand or more people, the Cherokee present their history and culture in a program called *"Unto these Hills"*. Using stories, songs, and dances as their means of expression, about 75 Cherokee actors present a show that magnificently explains the history of their Tribe. Every summer, thousands of people come to see this spectacular performance.

I want to tell you what I learned from this program. But first, it is important to note a sad fact of history, that President Andrew Jackson signed and enforced the Indian Removal Act of 1830 and most of the Cherokee and many other tribes from that part of the country had their land confiscated and were forcefully removed to the western territory. Many people refer to this removal as "The Trail of Tears."

I suggest you contact the Cherokee Nation website, where they present their whole story. I also highly recommend that you Google "Unto These Hills" and get tickets and go see their two-hour show.

The "Unto These Hills" program taught me three profound lessons about Cherokee people and about life. I took notes and this is what I remember.

> ➢ *First*, this lesson: "We are Cherokee—we all make mistakes."

I generalize this truth to all people. However, many people will not admit or own up to their mistakes. I thought this was an amazing truth to lead with.

> ➢ *Second*, this question: "We Cherokee people wondered why we were here and why we existed. So we *prayed* and asked the Creator for the answer."

Then seven "beings" appeared on the stage and they seemed about eight or nine feet tall. They all had distinct faces and different personalities.

And then came the answer: *"We came to help the people see what they could not see, and to see what they did not want to see."* The seven onstage 'beings' became seven different clans. Each one brought special understanding and insight to the people. They all had their important place in the history of the Eastern Band of the Cherokee Indians.

To me, learning how to perceive and understand what's good, right and true; and also removing denial is the reason we are here.

> ➢ *Third*, this promise: "It's now time for a new song and a new dance."

They were not going to dwell on the painful parts of the past. It was not in their best interests to go on a self-pity party.

***

This program reinforced in me, three profound truths:

➤ The first thing I learned is that we all make mistakes.

➤ Second, the reason we exist is to see and learn new things.

➤ And third, don't get stuck in resentment, but rather reinvent yourself and go for a new song and a new dance.

Chapter 34

We Live On Both Sides

One day many years ago, when I was employed as a counselor at Westwood High School in Mesa, Arizona, I said "goodbye" to Josie Enos, one of my Pima students.

She was heading off to class. But the minute she heard me say "goodbye", Josie immediately turned around and came back to me.

She looked right at me and said, "I want to teach you something about us Indians, Steve. *Indians don't say goodbye. We* say, *we'll see you.*"

My young student said this in a calm, matter-of-fact way but with such conviction that I have never forgotten it. It was a simple but great learning experience for me. Somehow, Josie conveyed something spiritual that made me feel that she was coming from a much deeper place.

Years later and a long way from home, the great Hawaiian singer Israel Kamakawiwoʻole, also known as "Bruddah IZ", explained in a song why Native people don't say goodbye. "I am not scared for myself—for dying—'cause I believe all this place is temporary. This is all one shell—because we Hawaiians, we live in both worlds. I don't know if you can relate to this—We live on both sides. So, it's kind of like if I went now, that's all right—I'd set the table for you guys, and keep the stew hot. We can't help

152

it—it flows through our body—it's in our veins—that's just the way it is."

For me, this simple explanation is enough to help me understand more fully why for most Native people saying goodbye doesn't feel right—or even make sense. In the "Indian Way" we will all meet again. Maybe that's why there is no Hawaiian word that just means goodbye. Instead, the word "Aloha" means "goodbye", and, at the same time, "hello".

In other words, for Native Americans and Hawaiians, there is no need for a word to say goodbye, because we will all see each other again!

Chapter 35

From Your Genes Right On Out

I first saw Dr. Taylor McKenzie at a conference at the University of Arizona in Tucson.

He was speaking on the subject of *identity*. Dr. McKenzie was Navajo, and he was one of the first Indian medical doctors in the United States. He addressed six hundred young Native students on the topic of culture and history. I recall him passionately pointing out that: *"Even if you can't fluently speak your native language and you are not as 'up' on your culture, as you would like to be, I want you to remember this—You are still Indian! The original spirit that was put in you is still there. You are Indian from your genes right on out."*

***

When it comes to the formation of our identity I have only one simple concept to share: the metaphor of the rope.

If you take a rope apart, you will find it to be made up of a lot of little ropes. This is what makes it strong, durable, and highly functional. How a *rope* is made helps me understand how I am made. Just like me, the rope has many different parts. I have many different identities and many different selves.

I have chosen to be positive about living in two worlds and accepting my multi-faceted, cultural identity.

When it comes to the rope, the Hopi have a fitting quote: "Take the good from the Hopi, and take the good from the non-Hopi, and wrap it all together like the strands of a lariat." Embracing the many strands of our diversity is what makes us strong in our power.

When I shared this story about the many strands that make up a rope with the Crow Nation in Billings, Montana, a young Native woman in the workshop opened her Bible. She freely shared this verse from Ecclesiastes 4:12: *"A triple-braided cord is not easily broken."*

She was comfortable with herself, and *strong enough in her power*, to share what she believed to be true with all of us. She took the good from her Tribe, the good from her American culture, and the good from her Faith, and wrapped it all together. She seemed very happy and comfortable with her multifaceted Native American identity.

We now live in a diverse, complex society. If you take America apart, you find that it's completely full of diversity. Embracing variety is what makes life interesting and it's also what makes us *strong in our power*.

Every day is different and full of change. As an Elder, I love growing and changing. No one day is the same as the day before, and every day is different. As Leander said: *"Appreciate every day."*

I personally feel that this is the best time to live. Why? Because the Creator wants me here now! This is what I choose to believe. Having a positive attitude is the key to everything. And in this book I have tried to explain how Spirit and Humor makes it possible for us to stay positive and live the good life.

Chapter 36

I Am More Than A Pima

I am sure you remember Leander, one of my very good friends from Salt River, and how much I learned from him through asking questions.

As an Elder, he, too, knew his O'odham language, culture and history.

When one day I asked Leander, "Why are you proud to be a Pima?" he thought for a while, then said . . .

"*. . . I am more than a Pima.*"

Then he went on to tell me how he had become a draftsman and worked in San Francisco for ten years. He added, "I also love sports, and I have studied all the great sport figures to see what makes them tick.

"I like to learn all kinds of things from all kinds of people. If I thought I would get all I needed from within the boundaries of this reservation, then I would be putting boundaries on my mind."

I thought that was a great answer, full of honesty, insight and wisdom.

Leander was a cosmopolitan man, and he also was keenly aware of American Indian history. He knew that losing 98 percent of the land, not to mention 75 percent of the language and culture, was not an easy burden to bear.

I wondered how he managed all of this—and how he remained so resilient. So one time I asked him: "What happens if you can't speak your traditional native language?"

He answered, with a matter of fact attitude, *"Then you do something else."*

One of the things I really admired and respected about Leander was how centered he was in his power and how at ease he was with his own formation of himself. I liked the way he celebrated life, completely comfortable with his multifaceted identity.

The Indigenous people of America lived here for thousands of years before the white man came. No one else has this distinction. As you may recall, my friend Howard Rainer pointed out that being Indian is "a state of mind." Exploring what this means is an interesting adventure. This happened to me when I went to Romania and found my roots. With open arms they embraced me. In order to go forward sometimes we need to look back and see where we came from.

Finding your tribal origins and knowing your cultural history is also a worthwhile endeavor for any Native American man or woman. Each person has a tribal or cultural identity. At this point in time, most people in America, including Native Americans, are a mixture of many different tribes and cultures. Each person also has his or her own unique *personal history*. I encourage you to have fun exploring your personal and ethnic identity. Discovering who you are as a modern day Indian is your responsibility. Defining who you are is something only you can do for yourself. It is nobody's business but your own.

The development of a person's identity and personality is an ongoing process. You are unique, and there is only one person like you. No one has ever been like you, and no one will ever be like you again. This is true, and in a way, each person is his or her own Tribe. There is only one you!

This is your life. I encourage you to live it. Put yourself right smack in the middle of it. Make you your project. Be your own best friend instead of your own worst enemy. See how good you could be. The world needs you. We are not alone and the Man in the Maze will be with each of us as we travel on this journey of life. The Hopi say, there is a life plan for everyone!

Here is what I tell myself as I travel on this journey of life. The following sayings ground me and help me be a better person:

> **What you are going to be, you are now becoming.**
> **You are here for a reason.**
> **The sun comes up every day so you can learn something.**
> **You grow a mind like you grow an ear of corn.**
> **The success of the future is half hidden in the now.**
> **You can be weak or *you can be strong in your power*.**
> **You get out of life what you put into it.**
> **It's your turn to live and take the culture apart and put it back together again.**
> **This is your time to do your dance and sing your song!**

Chapter 37

See How You Are

The Salt River people place a high priority on self-knowledge.

They use an expression that goes like this: *"See how you are."* It is a deceptively simple phrase but a noteworthy concept because it relates to our identity.

Life is about seeing, and often the hardest person for us to see is our-selves. The Salt River people recognize this. So when they see someone doing something that's off the mark, they note it. Their way of bringing it to that person's attention is to say: *"See how you are."*

It is a creative feedback expression that brings awareness to our behaviors. Often it is something we need to work on, correct, or change. It is an expression that gets our attention, and makes us look at ourselves.

For example, years ago I was buying a quart of beer at the convenience store. One of my students came into the store and saw me with the beer on the counter. As she passed me, she just looked at me and said: "See how you are."

When you think no one is looking, someone is looking. Someone sees how we are. Or, at least, they think they do. But a *word of caution* would be wise here; we need to be careful not to wrongly judge a person or a situation. Many times, the way things look on the surface is not at all how things really are underneath. Sometimes we make snap judgments.

It takes time to get to know a person, or a culture, and to really see what is going on underneath or behind the scenes. Our old friend Shakespeare said it best: "Things ought to be as they seem." However, in my experience I have learned that how things look on top, are often very different from the real situation. Here my guideline bears repeating- *Never prejudge, because it's hard enough to judge when you have all the facts*.

But there is one other very important piece of wisdom to consider here. Maya Angelou, a great American author and poet, who wrote the book 'I know Why the Caged Bird Sings', says this: *"When people tell you who they are—believe them."* There were many times I did not listen and made the wrong decision. All I have to say is, take your time, be careful and listen.

Chapter 38

My Biggest Shock Of All: Alcohol

Now, here is something I didn't see coming.

It was something that severely diminished my power and interfered with my song and dance. I never knew this could happen to me. Yet, it is all part of my story.

I sure didn't have all the facts on alcohol. I didn't really understand it until it hit home. Little did I know that alcohol would get me, but it did! And it happened only a few years ago, when I was 65 years old.

Heartache over a failed relationship dropped me into a deep depression. The mood turned into a full-bore resentment that I kept playing over and over again in my head. The mixed-up internal chatter in my head was taking me down fast. I could not sleep and I had no peace. So I started to drink at night so I could go to sleep, get some rest, escape my pain.

It started out ever so slowly, with just one drink. But quickly—and ever so cunningly—my intake progressed to two, three, and then four. In order to sleep, I had to have more and more alcohol. Before long, I graduated from wine to rum. I hate to admit it, but I even took liquor in my suitcase on business trips. As the disease took hold, I added sleeping pills—and, slowly but surely, something began to die in me.

I was no longer happy with myself—ever! Every morning I awoke in a fog of depression. An addiction is something that pins you down. You want to stop, but you can't. Mine hit me so hard, I went over the edge and was down for the count.

I knew this was wrong, but *I could not stop.* It was like I was in a *grinder* that was crushing me. I was locked up in the prison of alcohol.

My self-worth, and my desire to live, greatly diminished. I could not believe this was happening to me. Somehow a sinister, cunning, powerful, substance was now in charge of my life. I began to lose confidence in myself.

Once an addiction gets a grip on you, you're truly unable to see your way out. In my case, the way alcohol ruled my behavior and warped my thoughts was like a form of insanity.

Over the next two years it got progressively worse. Instead of being in charge, I began to give *all my power* away to alcohol. It got so bad, I started to totally lose all hope.

I finally owned up to the fact that I was in big trouble. I prayed, and I prayed. I agonized, and my spirit swirled downward in great turmoil about my situation. I got so discouraged and sank so low I couldn't even pray anymore. Out of desperation, I took a risk and confided in two of my friends. Sadly, they had no clue about how to help me. They just didn't get it. They were at a loss about what to tell me.

All I can say is God is Good, and with his infinite mercy, he took pity on me. He heard the prayers, after all. Some call it mercy; I call it *grace*!

And God chose a mysterious way to help me out of my no-win situation. Just when I was at the end of my rope, I got a late night phone call. To my surprise, it was an old Indian buddy from Salt River, a man I hadn't heard from for many years. He joked with me, and called me Lefty's son. (Years before, I had told him my real Dad was left handed, and he had nicknamed me "Lefty's son.") We talked for a little bit, and he kindly invited me to share a meal.

Chapter 39

The Stranger Became My Sponsor

When we met for lunch the next day, my friend showed up with two Native relatives.

I knew the first man, but the second man was a total *stranger* to me. He was a tall, thin, Native man from way up in the northern part of the country. The four of us ate, shared stories, and laughed. Then a glimpse of the answer I so desperately needed, unexpectedly appeared.

Out of the blue, in the midst of a conversation that had nothing to do with alcohol, addiction or drinking, this total stranger said, "You know, Steve, I drank for 20 years, and alcohol caused me and my family a lot of pain and misery. I lost my marriage, and because of my neglect as a parent, my son ended up in prison, and is still there today."

But, at the time we met, he had been sober for 13 years. I was a bit stunned by his self-disclosure. I didn't see any way he could have known I had a drinking problem. The subject of the conversation quickly changed, and we talked about other things.

Five days later, I received a phone call at 10 o'clock in the evening. It was from the total *stranger* that God used to help me turn my life around. He re-introduced himself and said he had gotten my number from his brother-in-law. Then he picked up right where he had left off in our first conversation, telling me, "Steve, you know, when I drank I would get to a point where I had to check myself into an emergency room in order to stay alive. When I hit bottom like that, one thought always kept coming back to my mind . . . I want to live, I don't want to die!"

I listened intently, all the time wondering, "Why is this man telling me all this stuff?"

But before I could even ask, he said, "Hey, I have to go. Let's keep in touch. I will talk to you another time."

What he said hit me hard, because I was already hitting bottom and was beginning to entertain thoughts of not wanting to be around here any more. Still, I couldn't stop drinking.

I continued drinking for five more days. I was feeling bad, deeply disappointed in myself. I was sad, lonely, and depressed. My alcoholism made me feel like a rat stuck in a trap. I felt blocked on all sides. Suddenly I remembered that the total stranger's number was on the caller I.D. of my cellphone. I found it, and got up enough nerve to call him.

I told him I needed to talk to someone because I was drinking every day and needed help. He instantly let me know he was glad that I had called. Without a second's hesitation, he told me, flat out, "Steve, it is good that you called me. The first step is *admitting* that you have a problem with alcohol."

I asked him if there was a place where we could meet and talk. He was a Pow Wow dancer and said meet me the next day at the Fort McDowell Pow Wow.

On the following afternoon, we sat and talked for a couple of hours. He invited me to an AA meeting the next evening. I went to the meeting, listened, and then went home and drank myself to sleep again. *I wanted to, but I just could not stop.* Something in me had crossed over the line, and I knew I was in big trouble.

So I called him again. He kindly agreed to meet with me at the Salt River Thanksgiving dinner.

After we ate, we went outside and sat in my car. We talked openly for a long time. I told him I was feeling really bad and that I was still drinking.

He said: *"Steve, You need to stop today."*

I said: "I can't, I just can't do it."

Then he said something that really got my attention: *"Steve, I am going to be blunt with you. You have a lot to lose. This is a progressive disease, and it will only get worse."*

He shared with me how he thought he was so smart and could deal with alcohol. He told me a horrible story of how he went out one night to drink and ended up getting drunk on the wrong side of town. How he got there, he had no idea. He said, "I thought I could handle alcohol; instead, that night, I got the worst beating of my life! Steve, you need to go to an Alcoholics Anonymous meeting tonight. There are a lot of meetings in the town where you live."

I shook my head, and told him, "I don't think so."

He did not go easy on me. He shook his head right back, and said: *"Go online and look."*

Little did I know, there were 12 meetings a week in my town. The help I so desperately needed was exactly one mile from my house. When I drove up to the meeting place that night it was cold and dark, but the lights were on. *I was never so happy to see lights on.*

I listened to the people talking, and it was all very new to me. But at the end of the meeting a man stayed and spoke with me. He said he'd tried three different recovery programs and at the end of each one was told the same thing—"Go to AA!" Then he gave me a warm, encouraging smile and said, "Steve, *I think you just need to give AA a try.* It worked for me, and I believe it will work for you."

A lady who overheard us added her thoughts. "Steve it is better to have some sleepless nights, then to ruin your life with alcohol. *Go cold turkey tonight, white knuckle it, and come to the AA meeting in the morning."*

I had never heard this "white-knuckle" expression before, but I quickly figured out it meant to suffer through the night and—no matter what—refuse to drink. That whole night I white knuckled it and did not sleep a wink! Then, since I was up anyway, I went to a morning meeting.

My white-knuckling night and the morning meeting that followed marked a turning point. From then on, I did exactly what was suggested. I went to 90 or more meetings in the next 90 days. And in the three months that followed I met some great people, heard some amazing stories . . . and stopped drinking!

It wasn't an easy journey. But I stuck with it and with God's help and the work of a good AA sponsor, I overcame the addictive pull of alcohol. Little by little, the need to drink went away, and I woke up each morning with a grateful heart. By the end of those 90 days I had begun to sleep well again, and I started enjoying a measurable amount of peace, happiness and freedom.

It's been a little over five years now, and I am grateful to report that I remain sober. And here's one of the most valuable "keys to sobriety" I've been given: one of the best ways to keep my sobriety is to *reach out and help those who are still suffering.* This simple action is my way of staying clean and sober. As they say in AA. *"If you want to keep it, you have to give it away."*

Of course, I also keep alive the memory of how unhappy my life used to be, and this is yet another aid to sobriety—I just don't want to ever go back to the frightening grip and depression of alcohol.

As I said earlier, I never understood this disease until it hit home. My personal experience with alcohol helped me truly empathize with other people who are suffering with this dreadful disease. After all, who is better qualified to understand the pain, despair, and loneliness, of an alcoholic than someone who's faced the demon of alcoholism head on?

Today I can honestly say: "If you go to the meetings and practice the 12 steps, your life will get better. And, in due time, you, too, will be able to help others who are still suffering.

I go to meetings regularly to this day. I go to be part of a support system for others, and I go because it reminds me of my primary purpose, which is to stay clean and sober.

Best of all, the 12 steps has helped me be a more spiritual person. My hard won recovery helped me really take to heart, things I heard at AA meetings, like the following: "I got into the steps and then the steps got into me." "The 12 steps can be reduced down to three things: Trust God, Clean house, Help others." "Honesty happens here." "We need to surrender to win." *Best of all, I made a lot of new friends and experienced a new design for living.*

At a Thanksgiving AA meeting in November of 2015 I received my five-year membership chip. Printed on it is this quote from the AA Big Book: *"Rarely have we seen a person fail who has thoroughly followed our path."*

The following words of truth were given to me by the total *stranger* who introduced me to AA and became my sponsor.

He said: "Steve, for a long time I did not know or understand it, but I now believe it's true: *"God uses people to help people."* My sponsor also told me: *"Not everyone gets to get sober"* and *"you don't have to drink, even if you want to."*

Recently, a Fort McDowell Elder shared this story at an AA meeting: "I have relatives who are drinking hard every day. I told them that if they keep it up, they could get in an accident, get hurt—or worse, end up in jail . . . or dead!

"I want you to know I am not telling you to stop drinking. You will have to decide that for yourself. I am only telling you what may happen if you continue."

There are two powerful lessons in this no-holds-barred story.

> ➤ I take away your dignity and weaken your self-respect when *I choose* for you.
>
> ➤ Only *you* have the power to *choose for you.*

This is what it means to be strong in your power.

One last thought. After my first two years of being sober and a member of AA, I shared my story with Josie Enos, the Salt River woman who, many years ago, told me that Indians don't say goodbye. When Josie heard my story, this is what she said. "You must have some strong ancestors who were praying and looking out after you."

What she shared made me humble. It also made me think.

Chapter 40

May Your Life Be Fulfilled Unto Old Age

The Hopi people realize that not everyone is blessed to live to a ripe old age.

Therefore, they weave this into their ceremony as they give a name to each newborn baby. As part of the blessing they recite these words: *"May your life be fulfilled unto old age."*

Now I would like to share with you some stories from Elders whose lives have been fulfilled unto old age.

Sometimes we don't even realize how fulfilled we are. One of my favorite examples of this was provided by a woman named Clara Nicholas, whose Indian name was Gray Owl.

Gray Owl told me that the young people in her community were having a youth council meeting and they wanted to know more about their history and their culture. The next morning a young girl phoned Gray Owl and said: "Last night, your name came up as one of the Elders who knows a lot about our people. Can you speak to our youth council?"

At this point in her story, Gray Owl smiled and admitted, "I was thinking to myself the whole time the young girl was speaking . . . "Why is she asking me? I am only 52 years old!"

Then it dawned on her, and Gray Owl 'got it'.

In her words: *"I woke up one morning, and discovered I was one of the Elders!"*

So, I guess that's how it happens. If you live long enough, you will become one of the Elders. And one of the best parts of becoming an Elder is that you indeed have in your experience a generous supply of life stories.

***

On a personal note, if you are an older person reading this book right now, I want to encourage you to write a book containing your favorite stories. You may be pleasantly surprised—if you start writing—at how many wonderful memories and funny stories will find their way into your manuscript.

Go ahead. Give it a try. Leave a legacy. If I can do it, you can, too. Put your life story into a book, and I guarantee it will bless you, your children and your friends. And it just might surprise you how many other people it may bless. You never know until you try!

***

Emma Lewis was one of the oldest and most respected Elders in the Salt River community. Mrs. Lewis would often speak to my Pima/Maricopa Culture and History class, saying things like, *"We are all traveling somewhere."* So, after class I asked her what she meant and this is what she said: *"We are all on a journey, and we are all traveling somewhere. The way we live our lives determines where we end up. We could end up in a dark, deep pit, or we can end up in a bright and beautiful place. This is what our people believed long before the white man came."*

***

A few years ago, I heard an old Indian man speak at a Native American Conference in Albuquerque, New Mexico. This is the viewpoint he shared:

"When you look around, have you noticed that there is something happening in America? *America is getting brown again*. Five hundred years ago, when Columbus came, everybody was brown. Now it's happening again. I call it *The Re-Browning of America*."

Then, the speaker encouraged all the young people to get a good education. He challenged their parents with these words: "Make sure your children stay in school. They have to get a good education, because they are going to be running this country."

(Years later, in a totally different setting, I heard something similar; *"You can't be running a million dollar business, with a ten-cent education."*)

On the same subject, Wendell Chino, then the Chairman of the Mescalero Apache Nation that is located south of Albuquerque, New Mexico spoke at an Indian education conference, and he too expanded on the importance of obtaining a great education. This is what he said, *"As you look around the country you see lots of serious problems. I want to encourage you to turn these problems around and make them into challenges.* **You're Needed!** *Get an education; Make a difference; Help your people."*

Wendell Chino didn't mince words. I admire how forcefully he spoke his convictions.

***

Here is what this Elder (me!) believes:

"The best thing about America is not what we are, it is *what we aspire to be.*

We are a great country, and we have done great things. But we have also made our fair share of mistakes.

In our country, there are now hundreds of people injured or killed in gun-involved shootings every day. I wonder how this can happen, because in the Indian way, we are all related. You are my relative! How can I kill or hurt my relative? And yet the spirit of Cain still lives.

Fortunately, *I believe that America is not done becoming America.* Our best years are still in front of us. It is our time to live, and as I've said several times throughout this book, it is our turn to take the culture apart and put it back together again. My goal is to leave this camp ground a little better than I found it. I hope this is your goal too!

***

In this book, I have spoken several times about Analita Smith, and what an amazing Elder she was. Toward the end of her life, Analita had to be hospitalized and was placed under careful medical supervision. When she came back home from the hospital, she began to prepare her funeral. She picked out her songs and decided what she wanted the congregation to know about her.

I, along with *hundreds* of other people, attended her funeral service. The chapel was completely filled and there were many people standing outside, so the doors were left open to allow them to hear the service.

Analita had thought of everything, and she made sure to leave careful instructions.

Above all, this was the message she wanted us to know: *"I am leaving this garden in your hands. It's up to you now to take care of it."*

I knew just which garden she meant. For many years, Analita worked at the Youth Home in Salt River. The orphaned and abandoned children who were boarded there didn't have homes in the community. *They were her garden.* I had visited her many times at the Home, and she always had me talk to the children. The role she played in their lives, and the message Analita left us, was very powerful. She wanted to make sure that somebody would continue to *tend her garden by stepping up to* take care of these kids after she was gone.

All of us 'Elders' have our own kind of garden. Oftentimes it is our grandchildren. This is why I wrote this book. I thought it would help my grandchildren know who their grandpa was, how much he loved them, and how much he wanted what was best for their future.

It doesn't matter which culture you live in. In this country of ours, there are many different Worlds. As you get older, I encourage you to make the most of being an Elder. Take in good wherever you can find it. Just be your beautiful self and have some fun with it. Then, pass what is good on to others.

So, regardless of your age, I encourage you to think about *your* garden. It's never too soon, or too late, to ask yourself: "What would I like to be remembered for?" What can I do to make this world a better place?

I wish for you two things: May your life be fulfilled unto old age, and may you be blessed with a beautiful garden!

Chapter 41

The Summing Up Ceremony

I clearly remember when a Native man from the state of Washington spoke at our college and told us that on his trip to visit us he had bought a beautiful necklace for his daughter.

"When I return home," he said, "I will say to my daughter, 'I have a gift for you, my daughter. *It's a good luck necklace*. It will help you get anything you want. *All you have to do is work for it*'."

I like the simple lesson in this story. The gardens we grow—the things we accomplish in our lives—all depend on us. Youth or Elder, we get what we are willing to work for. Saying this another way: In this life, you get out of it what you put into it. (The Earth is Round)

I have learned, first-hand, that people who are successful aren't any smarter than the rest of us, they are just willing to work harder.

There is a Hopi saying: "When you're planting a row of corn, every once in a while you need to look back to see if your row is straight." As a farm boy, I know the meaning of this quote.

As I look back, I see that I have made my share of mistakes. But the very act of looking back helps us decide to change and make adjustments so we can return to the right path and move forward. There have been many times over the years when I have had to humble myself and start over again.

I am also amazed at how much the experience of living in two worlds has enriched my life—and how all the people I met, and all the stories they have shared—have shaped my life.

I have learned so much from my Native American friends and students.

***

One piece of wisdom that's worth repeating is the following Hopi saying: "Take the good from the Hopi, and take the good from the non-Hopi, then wind all these good things together like the strands of a lariat."

I now believe that respecting and carefully embracing diversity is what makes us strong in our power. It's what I have tried to do as I travel on my journey. Bringing together the best of both worlds has helped me find meaning and formulate my philosophy of life. I am so glad I can share all these things with you.

***

Many Tribes have a spiritual belief that helps their people be more conscious about the consequences of their actions. They call it *Seven Generations*.

The idea is to imagine the consequences of our actions that may be felt far into the future in a way that helps us be more mindful of how we treat the Earth, and how we treat each other in the present moment.

This cautionary Tribal belief reminds us that whatever we do today should be carefully thought through with a view to seeing what impact it might have on each of the seven generations yet to come. Taking such a long view helps us to consider seriously the footprint we want to leave upon this Earth.

Seattle, who was the Chief of the Suquamish Indians wrote a letter to the President in Washington D.C. In part the letter stated: "How can you buy or sell the sky or the land. The idea is strange to us. Every part of the earth is sacred to our people." (I encourage you to find and read the whole letter) The city of Seattle is named after this great Chief, who also said, *"The Earth does not belong to us. We belong to the Earth."*

In my opinion, Mother Earth does not seem to be feeling too well these days. Vital natural habitats are seriously threatened. We need to remember and honor this basic truth: "Animals can live without people, but people cannot live without animals."

It's time to take a stand, for the health and wellness of our planet. We are all related! Let's protect our Mother Earth with everything we've got, and make it a good day to die, so that the Earth can live, for many generations.

Remember, too, what Mr. Ronnie Lupe, the White Mountain Apache leader said: "In our Apache language, the word for *earth* and the word for *mind* are the same word." (Ni')

To me, this quote illustrates why the *land* and the way we *think* about the land are so deeply interconnected. It's why I so passionately believe: "When we lose our Earth, we lose our mind, and when we lose our mind, we lose our way."

When this happens we end up empty. Viktor E. Frankl calls this empty space an existential vacuum, with no meaning and no purpose. As a result of this emptiness we become angry, depressed and then we attempt to numb our painful confusion with drugs and alcohol.

On this journey of life, I have learned that we must never give up on ourselves. In this life there are many new starts. No matter what happens we must stay on the good road and keep on going. As we travel through the maze of life there are many twists and turns. Sometimes the path is so narrow, we can't even see it. Remember, Talking God is with us. We are not alone. In times like this, I remember one of my favorite verses from the Old Testament: "Weeping may endure for a night, but joy cometh in the morning." *The magic light of the morning sun sets the stage for a brand new day*. It's another chance to enjoy life, give thanks, and be *strong in our power*.

So *appreciate every day*, because, before you know it, it will be time to go!

Chapter 42

Until We Meet Again

Many years ago, I heard a Native American leader, from an Eastern Tribe, who was asked, "What is your philosophy?"

He answered with four words that I've never forgotten: *"Enjoy life, give thanks."*

The older I get, the more I want to be the kind of Elder who exemplifies that simple but profound, philosophy. Those four words remind me of this quote from Meister Eckhart, a fourteenth century philosopher and theologian: "If the only prayer you ever said was 'thank you,' that would be enough."

Writing this book, *Living in Two Worlds*, has helped me fully grasp the meaning and value of my life. What I know to be true and important I have now shared with you.

I have come to the conclusion that enjoying life, giving thanks, and being strong in our power are all closely related. All three complement and positively strengthen one another. They are like the triple-braided cord (the lariat or rope) that is not easily broken. You cannot properly do one without including the other two.

Living in two worlds has given me dual citizenship. I have been doubly blessed with two different perspectives. The spirituality and humor from both worlds profoundly enriched my life.

I am especially grateful for all the Native American people who have graciously shared their lives with me. I am a very blessed man!

I look forward to what's in front of me with a positive attitude, and I look back with these wonderful Native American memories:

> - My friend Judum and how our lifetime friendship richly blessed me.
> - The way Analita's wisdom is woven into my life and makes me happy.
> - How the Man in the Maze, and the Native American flute, continue to be such valuable metaphors for life.
> - The Hopi perspective on clowns and how they do skits on life as it should not be.
> - Chief Dan George, and the inspiring words of Chief Yellow Lark's favorite prayer.
> - I will never forget my powerful experience in the Navajo Sweat Lodge, and receiving the Prayer Song that is a blessing for everyone.
> - I also cherish the stories of Changing Woman, and the Navajo ceremony about "The Baby's First Laugh."
> - And of course I will always remember "Unto These Hills," and the three powerful lessons I learned from the Cherokee.

I must now also say thank you to my 'ten professors', all my grandchildren, who range in age from five months to 15 years as I write this book.

I want each of you children to know that I will love you forever. I want the best for each and every one of you. I believe in you, and I strongly encourage you to believe in yourselves, and to love and help each other. Oh yes, I also want you to know one more thing that Analita said: *"Make your parents proud!"*

I want all of you grandchildren to know that it was my love for you- and your love for me- that gave me the power to write this book. I hope these stories about humor and spirit will help you appreciate life and *triumphantly* do your dance and sing your song.

I can't wait for you to tell me all about it someday.

Well, it looks like it's time to go. I never was very good at saying goodbye. So, I will just do it the Indian way:

"I'll see you again someday." Until we meet again: *"Enjoy Life, Give Thanks!"* This is my Woozhii Wish for you, and for the whole world, too!

Remember, your Woozhiiness is Your Goodness, Your Playfulness, and Your Friendliness. All God's children got Woozhii!

Just work from your beautiful Woozhii heart. May your Woozhii live big time! Thanks for allowing me to share my story.

And the last thing I want to say is this: "World, don't mess with my Woozhii! Why? Because "This Kid is Good, Aye!"

About The Author

Steve Saffron is a Motivational Keynote Speaker who has delivered leadership and professional development programs to America for 25 years.

He is a *"Meaning Maker & Cycle Breaker."* Steve's seven topics are all about relationship building, teamwork, and positive attitude. In a most creative way, you will learn how to grow professionally and build a positive work climate.

Steve received an Associate of Arts degree from Mesa Community College, and later earned both a Bachelor's degree in Sociology and a Master's degree in Counseling from Arizona State University.

He began his Indian education career in 1972, at Alchesay High School, in Whiteriver, Arizona. In 1974, Steve worked in the Indian Program in the Mesa public schools.

In 1975, he was hired as a professor and counselor—and later as Director of Indian Services—at Scottsdale Community College (SCC), where he worked for 30 years, doing everything from counseling, to community outreach, to designing and teaching a Personal Development Class for Native American students. He credits many of his most innovative teaching tools to the wisdom he gleaned from Native people. When Steve began at SCC the Indian Services Program con-sisted of one faculty member (himself) and 27 Native American students.

Many years later, when Steve retired from the college, the American Indian Program had a staff of five people and about 500 Native American students. Both increases reflected the hard work, and determined leadership Steve and the Salt River Indian Community brought to his department.

In 1985, fresh from a sabbatical, Steve created the first course on Friendship, and also the first Laughter, Humor and Play class in the entire United States. Both classes were for full college credit and were open to all students. For 10 years, both classes remained some of the most popular courses on campus.

During his long career Steve Saffron has been recognized with many awards, including, "The Phoenix Choice Award" and also the "Raising the Bar in a Time of Change" award, from the National Head Start Association.

He is especially proud of two other awards: The *"Devoted and Distinguished Service Award"* for over 20 years of educational service to the Salt River Pima Maricopa Indian community; and the *"American Indian Excellence in Leadership Award"* he received in 2012, when the Phoenix Indian Center honored him for being a long-time friend of the American Indian Community.

Since leaving the college, Steve has launched a successful career as a professional speaker. His humorous and motivational speeches, along with his engaging and uplifting trainings, have allowed him to share his positive message all across the country.

Steve often presents programs at Native American gatherings and has also been honored to be a keynote presenter at various companies and organizations around the country, including Head Start conferences annually for the past 25 years.

You can learn more about Steve and his professional speaking topics by visiting his two websites and/or contacting him by E-mail:

➤ www.thekidisgood.com

➤ www.buildapositiveworkclimate.com

➤ E-mail: Steve@thekidisgood.com